D1591146

WITHDRAWN

DEATH OF A
ROLLING STONE
The Brian Jones Story

858378

WEST PALM BEACH PUBLIC LIBRARY

DEATH OF A
ROLLING STONE

The Brian Jones Story

by Mandy Aftel

Delilah BOOKS

DISTRIBUTED BY THE PUTNAM PUBLISHING GROUP

NEW YORK

921
Jones

Copyright © 1982 Mandy Aftel

A Delilah Book
Delilah Communications Ltd.
118 E. 25 Street
New York, New York 10010

ISBN: 0-933328-37-0
Library of Congress Catalog Card Number: 82-71196

Manufactured in the U.S.A.
First printing 1982

All rights reserved. No part of this book may be reproduced or
transmitted in any form or by any means, electronic or mechanical,
including photocopying, recording or by any information storage and
retrieval system, without permission in writing from the Publisher.

P H O T O   C R E D I T S :

Front cover photos: Gered Mankowitz
 Syndication International *(inset)*

Back cover photo courtesy of D.M. Templeton and John Mars

Photo of Mandy Aftel by Tim O'Leary

Collection of Tom Beach: *pp. 20, 34, 54,
 65, 78, 109, 122, 135, 151, 206*

Collection of Alan Betrock: *pp. 79, 81*

Gered Mankowitz: *pp. 1, 4, 21, 62, 77,
 124, 130, 168, 188*

Courtesy of Linda (Lawrence) Leitch: *pp. 70, 83-84 (postcards)*

Courtesy of D.M. Templeton and John Mars: *14*

Syndication International: *pp. 2, 6, 13, 43, 72, 89, 97, 102, 103,
 104, 111, 146, 150, 158, 187, 199, 200, 204, 205, 208*

Book Design: Ed Caraeff

JUL   1983

For Slava

About The Author

Mandy Aftel lives in Berkeley, California with her husband and two-year old daughter. She is a psychotherapist who specializes in artists and writers.

P R E F A C E

This is the story of Brian Jones based upon the recollections of those who knew him best.
This is not a history of the Rolling Stones.

WHO WAS THE PRIVATE BRIAN JONES? WHO WAS the person behind the world's fantasies? What was at the center of this myth? How did he cope with so much so fast? What happens to those who live in the center of a whirlwind? How real can they be, even to themselves? I needed to know the answers to these questions.

I only knew about two other people who tried to write a book about Brian Jones. The first died and the second gave up. I had heard rumors of others as well. What could be so difficult? Janis Joplin, Jimi Hendrix, Jim Morrison were the subjects of biographies. Why not Brian? As I began interviewing, I discovered the major problem: no one wanted to talk about his life. When a friend dies at twenty-seven, in a terrible state of physical and emotional deterioration, it is not a subject that invites discussion. Some of Brian's friends clearly didn't want to talk because they felt guilty about what they could have or should have done. Others seemed fearful that I was going to make more trash out of an already seamy and scandalous life. And then there were those who simply found it too painful to dig up the old hurtful feelings.

Although I had never published, in 1974, I decided to write a biography of Brian Jones. I talked to several writers in the Bay Area who had written articles on the Rolling Stones, and after many phone calls met with (the late) Ralph Gleason. He was encouraging and made me feel that with hard work I could finish the book and see it published.

After several leads from a FM radio station, I flew to Los Angeles to find people who had known Brian. I had heard that John Lennon was living in Los Angeles, and called on Tony King at Capitol Records to try to arrange an interview with him. Tony said curtly that he didn't think that John had known Brian very well. I explained that I had wanted to speak to John Lennon because I thought he had known Brian, not because he was John Lennon. At that Tony warmly apologized, "I'm terribly sorry; I misjudged you. So many people just want to meet John." As it turned out, *Tony* had known Brian and I did my first interview with him.

Meanwhile, I collected hundreds of rock publications, read all I could about Morocco (which was a very special place for Brian), and tried to interview relevant rock people when they were in the Bay Area. I wrote letters (all unanswered) to Mick Jagger and the rest of the Stones explaining my book and telling them I'd be in England for the summer. With nothing more than a few phone numbers, all my savings, and an extensive list of names and places, I left for London in early August, 1974.

My first call was to the Stones' first secretary who had reportedly been close to Brian. She refused an interview, preferring that nothing ever be written about Brian. Equally encouraging, she informed me that Mick Jagger and Keith Richard would *never* agree to talk to me. I felt a failure.

I arranged to meet with Anna Menzies, the Rolling Stones' current secretary, later that week; I hoped she would provide me with important names and phone numbers. Already I had looked up what seemed like a million numbers in the London telephone book with no success (almost all names are listed by initials).

Fortunately, before leaving for England, I had gotten Keith Richard's home address in London. I decided to go to his house and ask him if he wanted to talk about Brian. Not without trepidation, I knocked on the door. Keith answered. I had interrupted a birthday party for his son. Keith was wearing black pants, a black shirt and had a big tooth hanging on a chain around his neck. When I told him who I was and what I was doing, he said, yes, he would talk to me and to set up a time through Anna Menzies. The interview looked within reach.

I went through my list of names with Anna at our meeting. She gave me a few phone numbers but made me promise that I would never drop in and "pester" Keith again. She assured me that *she* would arrange an interview with him.

Interviews started falling into place. Most people spoke openly and emotionally about Brian—relieved to share memories once they were certain that I was not exploiting Brian. I did everything but backflips to convince people of my sincerity. And people talked. At the end of an interview, some people said they felt relieved, unburdened, somehow more resolved after talking to me about Brian.

I always offered my interviewees the option of keeping the tape if they regretted anything they had said. I showed them how to operate the tape recorder so they could control what was being recorded. This basic respect for them eased communication and lifted barriers between us. Hardly anyone asked if I had a publisher and when one did I told the truth—that this was my first book and I didn't have a contract. Although I feared admitting this might discredit me, it didn't seem to make much difference. Rock 'n' roll people are basically working-class kids turned stars who attach little importance to academic credentials. Being a woman working in male-dominated, groupie-proliferated rock 'n' roll world was an advantage. Most of the men I spoke to were friendly and open to a woman interviewer.

My visit was nearly over and the Keith Richard interview had not yet been arranged. I felt Anna was stalling me, so with fear in my heart, I returned to Keith's house. A voice through the intercom told me that he would return in a few hours. Freezing, I stood across the street on the bank of the Thames waiting for three hours until he and Anita returned. They did let me in and Keith went upstairs. After two more hours of waiting and playing with his kids, the doorbell rang. It was Anna Menzies. She scowled in my direction. Finally, after talking some business with her, Keith reappeared. "I really do want to talk to you about Brian," he said. "We are moving tomorrow. Call Anna for directions to our new house and we will do the interview tomorrow at eight."

Elated, I phoned Anna the next morning: "Keith wants you to give me directions to his new house because we are going to do the interview tonight."

"I won't give them to you . . . er . . . ah . . . Lovey, I just don't have them. Why don't you call back tomorrow?"

I greeted my morning interviewee, Ian ("Stew") Stewart, in a frenzy. Ian has played piano on many of the Stones' albums and is now the group's road manager. I told him of my plight. Since Keith had described me to Ian as "sincere," he gave me the new address. That night, I interviewed Keith for four hours. He was extremely polite and helpful to me.

I returned to California happy, forty hours of interview tapes in my bag. I quickly taught myself to type and transcribed all the interviews. Then began the two-year haul of actually writing the book. I made numerous wall charts of facts, trying to put together Brian's life. I remained in contact with Linda (Lawrence) Leitch and her husband, Donovan, and went to live with them in the Mojave Desert for four months. It was there that I wrote the bulk of the book.

I WOULD LIKE TO THANK ALL THE PEOPLE I INTER-
viewed who so openly shared their past with me, spoke
movingly of Brian and often communicated great faith in
this undertaking. I would especially like to thank the late
John Appleby, Al Aronowitz, Jo Bergman, George
Chkiantz, Bo Diddley, Kathy Etchingham, Jim Carter-Fae,
Christopher Gibbs, the late Ralph Gleason, Doug Glenn,
Giorgio Gomelsky, Ellen Grehan, Richard Hattrell, Jon
Hendricks, Glyn Johns, Peter Jones, Tony King, Alexis
Korner, Violet Lawrence, Donovan Leitch, Linda Law-
rence Leitch, Ronny Money, D. A. Pennebaker, Keith
Richard, Debby Scott, Ian Stewart, Salli Stevenson, and
Penelope Tree.

I would like to thank Chris Cousins for her editorial
assistance and express my appreciation to Mildred Ash
and Robin Lakoff for their support and encouragement.
Special appreciation to Theo Green and the Brian Jones
Memorial Fan Club for their support. I am grateful, more
than words can say, to Linda Lawrence Leitch for her gen-
erosity and kindness. And last, my heartfelt appreciation to
Slava, without whom this never would have been possible.

> To have fame
> and youth at once
> is too much for a
> mortal
>
> —*Schopenhauer*

I

Brian Jones was the first
Rolling Stone. Without him there simply would have been
no Rolling Stones. Brian founded, named, and promoted
the group. During his last seven years Brian learned to play
thirty instruments, scored a movie, recorded an album of
ethnic Moroccan music, fathered at least three illegitimate children, was busted twice, scarred permanently by
police harassment, and was thrown out of the Rolling
Stones. What causes life to take such a downward course
in a beautiful and brilliant boy? Why had he deteriorated
so appallingly before the age of twenty-five?

One could say that it was the deadly progression of
dooming events: his father's lack of acceptance of him;
losing the band to Mick, Keith, and Andrew Oldham; the
loss of Anita, his girlfriend, to Keith; to his rifts with the
law and the continual threat of being incarcerated; and,
finally, the drugs themselves, which made him more
afraid of people and less able to function.

It is, perhaps, easier to assign blame, and definitely
more reassuring. Mick has blamed the drug busts; Anita
has blamed Mick and Keith; Brian's father has blamed the
newspapers. But it is more complicated than this. Life
always is. It never yields answers—only refines itself to
better questions.

Brian Jones, the first rock 'n' roll casualty—The
Golden Boy of The Golden Age: The Sixties—died on July
3, 1969 at twenty-seven. As Pete Cole, London journalist
said, "He [Brian] was made and destroyed by the times in
which he lived." In the book *Woodstock Census,* over a

thousand people were asked to define the sixties. One answer to the question of whatever happened to the sixties was, "When the deaths of Joplin, Brian Jones, and Hendrix occured, I felt very sad. It seemed that this was an irrevocable ending of an era." (It is interesting that Jim Morrison of the Doors died—at age twenty seven—exactly two years after Brian, on July 3, 1971.)

What made the sixties? Some said it all boiled down to money: so much economic freedom was then taken for granted. And money breeds leisure and leisure breeds the arts. If this premise is true, life is nothing more than a response to the times that shape it. Was Brian Jones, therefore, any more than a response to the times that shaped *him*? Was it enough to be just that? The fact that Brian was white and male—the Everyman—makes it somehow easier to study him than Janis Joplin, a woman, or Jimi Hendrix, who was black. It seems to me more than mere coincidence that none of these three gifted, self-destructive, flamboyant, vulnerable people survived past 1970.

Brian never reached his "creative potential," a very sixties notion. He was the quintessential under achiever. Despite his raw intelligence and talent he had no discipline to ·shape it into something tangible. It is sad indeed that Brian can ultimately be summed up as a profound waste. Probably no one was more aware of it than he and more torn-up by that knowledge.

Much of what Brian actually lived through was an emblem for the sixties. The acceleration of rock 'n' roll. The shoot to the top, out of your realm, into a world presence without formal training or advanced education. Dabbling with the mind expansion of drugs; the simultaneous joy of "cosmic" consciousness as well as the dreaded paranoia and abject fear of a "bad trip." The drug busts, brushes with the law, and the resulting hatred and fear of the Establishment. The change in sexual mores: Brian had many illegitimate children, and openly lived with women at a time when society expected most women to be virgins when they married. Could you call that too much too soon? Could you call the whole decade that?

The sixties supported certain values with a feverish pitch. It was not cool to be "bored," be a boring person, live a boring life. The Who summed it up in "My Generation": "I hope I die before I get old" (because it's boring to get old). As Brian said in an interview in *Everybody's* magazine when talking about his childhood: ". . . I guess that I knew that I was going to be interested in music early on—and that was because I quite honestly didn't feel much of an urge to do anything else. I just thought about the different sorts of jobs and rejected them because I knew I'd be *bored* [italics mine] stiff."

Later, Brian talked about why he didn't like sports such as soccer or cricket. "I couldn't stand being *bored*" [italics mine]. It's safe to say Brian was never bored—desperate, terrified, thrilled, overwhelmed—but *never* bored.

To many, the sixties represented innocence, being open, letting it "all hang out." Brian certainly was open to new artistic and personal experiences, to whatever came his way. This was especially true of his music. As Toby Goldstein of *ROCK* magazine said, "Brian Jones was not one to miss out on anything. To indulge his musical cravings, he learned to play all the odd instruments that gave the Stones' early and middle period recordings unique colorations. After basic rhythm guitar, the harmonica was first—it is widely agreed that Brian was one of the top harpists amongst the new wave British bands. His desire to play was unstoppable. The 13-minute 'Going Home' from *Aftermath* not only illustrates Jones' excellence on the harp, it also taught Mick Jagger a hell of a lot of the catch phrases he used playing harmonica on 'Midnight Rambler' cut three years later. To elaborate on Jagger-Richard compositions with tones its composers might not have imagined, Brian would pick up a dulcimer ('Lady Jane'), a sitar ('Paint It Black'), an electronic instrument panel (throughout *Satanic Majesties*), even a comical saxophone ('Something Happened to Me Yesterday'). Plus organ, piano, harpischord, marimbas, bells, and various percussion instruments. . . . He gave the Rolling Stones instruments as colorfully diverse as peacock feathers, and as proud."

Another prevalent "statement" during the sixties was in the importance of personal expression. Brian made a statement to the world through his style of clothes and how he wore them. He loved to dress up and collect ornaments. Panoply attracted him. He had said that uniformity in males frightened him. He pushed this notion, within the realm of clothing, to its androgynous limit, coming on stage festooned with antique brooches and enameled Berber necklaces, scarves billowing from his knees and elbows. He elevated dressing to an art form which soon caught on with the bead-incense-and-bell generation.

"When it came to lifestyles, Brian wrote the definition of the English pop star . . ." said Al Aronowitz, American journalist. "Brian was always a dandy. In the end, he was like a princeling who had run out of toys to play with. Once he kept a box-score of his women and it added up to sixty-four in one month, a pace which didn't allow for the luxury of a one night stand. That was all right for Brian. He used to find them waiting in his bathroom and in his closets and in his bed and he'd take them two at a time."

Brian Jones grew up in Cheltenham Spa, which Keith Richard fittingly described as a "very genteel old ladies' resting place; very pretty in its way, but dullsville." Cheltenham, at the edge of the Cotswolds, is about one hundred miles west of London. Regency architecture dominates the town: massive sheet-white houses, Doric columns practically everywhere; neat rows of windows, geometric and precise, with overhanging awnings of delicate ironwork. Replicas of the Erectheon Caryatids decorate the town's most popular shopping street, Montpelier Walk. Massive trees bower the spacious streets. In the center of town are the Imperial Gardens where flowers grow scrupulously according to some Cheltenhamian master plan. The atmosphere is almost holy. I visited Cheltenham on the August bank holiday. Everything was closed, including the flower shops. Yet the idea of picking a flower from one sacred formation was unthinkable.

Cheltenham's physical trappings articulate the intense civic pride even her young residents feel. They are proud that there are no unsightly parking meters because the city features a meterless parking system. They are proud of the imposing Regency houses and the grandiose streets and squares called Victoria, Wellington, and Trafalgar. They are proud that Cheltenham has two public (equivalent of private in America) schools and colleges. Cheltenhamians do not confine their concern for appearance to the town's landscape. They are extremely self-conscious and strive to do the "proper thing." They occupy themselves with propriety to the point of lifting their little finger when they drink tea, a mannerism Brian Jones assumed when the spirit moved him. Much of Brian's personality was formed in Cheltenham and although he often loathed these parts of himself, he could never divorce himself from them.

In Cheltenham, Brian was primarily exposed to a middle-class existence of propriety, respectability and education. Brian learned at an early age that these were the criteria for gaining his parents' love and the community's acceptance. At the same time, he was filled with the need for creative excitement and rebellion. These two parts vied with each other from late adolescence until his death.

Cheltenham did not take well to one of her boys becoming a Rolling Stone. Many of Mrs. Jones' friends stopped seeing her, and when by chance they met her at the supermarket, they stared and whispered. Brian's sister, Barbara, had great difficulty finding a job: after her graduation from Teacher's College, Barbara listed her school as a reference only to find that the headmistress was pointing out Barbara's brother as a drug addict and an undesirable. Brian's enraged father, Lewis Jones, demanded to know why the headmistress had offered this irrelevant information. The headmistress replied that she felt it was her Christian duty.

From this popular image, one would hardly suspect that on his visits home Brian's first request was always a glass of milk and a cucumber sandwich. Or that he read the Bible for hours. Or how devoted he was to a double-decker wooden toy bus, equipped with lights and horn that his father had made for him when Brian was little. Even when he was a successful Rolling Stone, on every home visit Brian pushed the toy around and flashed the lights.

Brian, age three. Cheltenham, 1945.

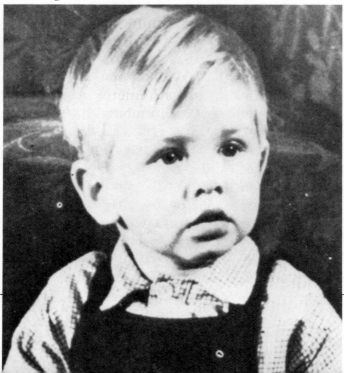

Lewis Brian Jones was born into a musical household on February 28, 1942. His mother, Louise, taught piano; his father, Lewis, a Welshman, sang in a chorus and dabbled with piano and organ. His sister Barbara, three years younger, was to become a skillful pianist and violinist. At an early age, Brian learned piano theory and sight-reading from his mother.

As a fee-paying student at Dean Close Grammar School, Brian excelled in music and English. For his First Form (seventh grade) English class, he had to write a new creative piece every week. Brian, however, made up a space story in serial form, adding a new chapter weekly. This delighted his teacher, who could hardly wait to read the next installment. After graduation Brian went on to the classy Cheltenham Grammar School. Although Brian was a good student he preferred listening to records and the radio. He liked to improvise, whistling along with early jazz tunes such as "When the Saints Go Marching In" and "Muskrat Ramble." "As things turned out," Lewis Jones said of Brian, "had he devoted as much time to his studies as he did to music, I think he would have been a brilliant scholar. He had an I.Q. of 135." Ian Stewart, the Stones' road manager stated, "Brian was brilliant at school. He had a very, very good brain, even better than Mick's." Richard Hattrell, a hometown friend, recalled, "He was a rebel without a cause but when examinations came he was brilliant."

While at the grammar school, Brian led a rebellion against the prefects and as a result he was suspended for awhile. A few months later a girlfriend of his became pregnant and he dropped out of school. Brian wanted her to have an abortion but she insisted on having the baby. Although the mother and child continued to live in Cheltenham, she refused to have anything to do with Brian. The scandal alienated Brian from his classmates. "He didn't want to continue school because the whole image was blown." Linda Lawrence, who later lived with Brian for two years, explained, "Everything was messed up. They looked down on him because he got a girl pregnant and he was uncomfortable at school."

From that time on, Brian existed in a life entirely different from the one which his parents must have expected of him. His father was extremely disappointed when Brian quit school. Naturally enough Lewis Jones, a hard-working aeronautical engineer with Cheltenham's largest employer, the Dowty Group, had planned a university education and a professional career for Brian. Lewis felt that Brian's rejection of his career scheme caused friction: "The problem between Brian and myself was not so much one of personality as ambition." One wonders if it was only Brian's career choice that led Lewis Jones to remark, "Brian exasperated me beyond measure in his younger days, but my wife and I never ceased to love him."

All children want to please and feel accepted by their parents, and Brian Jones was no different. All his life he looked for evidence that—in his own way—he had finally pleased his parents. Conforming to the professional Cheltenham tract was antithetical to Brian's nature, yet he longed for the nod, the wink, the few words that said "You belong." The words never came.

Brian's parents also tried to shield his sister from his negative influence. Brian and Barbara's estrangement was evidenced in a final and terribly strange detail. Barbara had a pen-pal in the United States, a woman Brian had met on a tour in 1964. The two women exchanged letters for eight years. When Brian died, Barbara sent her pen-pal newspaper clippings about his death, as if a famous stranger had died. "Doesn't sound very personal, does it?" the pen-pal remarked to me.

Brian wanted very much to be close to his father—but not on his father's terms. Even after Brian had become a successful Rolling Stone he still sought his father's approval. "Brian would sit up for two days and nights writing and rewriting letters to his parents," Keith Richard told me. "What Brian wanted was an admission, at last, (that no matter how he'd done it) he'd gotten his own thing together. . . . He'd come back from visits with his parents and would always say he couldn't communicate with them. Out of all the Stones, Brian was a lot more conscious of his background and what his family thought of him than the rest of us."

In response to the lack of approval given him in his childhood, Brian developed an intense drive to succeed. Richard Hattrell felt that Brian wanted desperately to succeed in music to prove something to his father: "His father never tried to understand what Brian wanted, which was why Brian tried to make a success of what began as an interest, developed into an obsession, and finally became a career. Once, after a performance in 1961 at which the Stones played for free, Brian came back to the pad and practiced all night until he literally fell asleep over his guitar. He vehemently played guitar. He wanted to be *the* best."

In an interview given the day after Brian's death, Lewis Jones indicated that he felt a turning point in this tenuous father-son relationship occurred the night Brian telephoned from London, after months of silence, to say he wanted to talk to his parents about a band he was starting: "To me," Lewis Jones said, "this was evidence that in spite of our early disagreements, he still regarded me as his confidant. He came to Cheltenham to see us and was full of his ambition for the future. He appeared to have found what he was looking for, a chance to become a competent jazz musician. It was on this occasion that he first mentioned a group of people he called the Rolling Stones. From that moment on there was a complete and lasting reconciliation."

To conclude that Brian regarded Lewis as a confidant implies a state of mind uncluttered enough to make choices between acceptance and rejection. Brian was unable to make these choices. His needs for love and a demonstration of affection were too great to risk rejection from anyone. For Brian, "openness" was an involuntary response; he was like a fisherman who casts his line hoping it will make contact.

By 1960, when Brian was no longer in school, he spent many hours hanging out with beatniks at local coffee bars. The informal atmosphere was a relief from the rest of Cheltenham. Two years earlier Roy Sellick had transformed 56 High Street, Cheltenham, from a dismal dark place into the El Flamenco coffee bar, complete with coconut matting, tree-trunk tables and benches, and expresso machines. The "El Flam," principal meeting place for the young, began filling up at 8:00 P.M. and remained crowded until the early morning hours. Customers often helped themselves to their own food and also helped Roy in the kitchen. Here Brian could pick up messages, find out about parties or have a late-night snack.

Cheltenham might seem an incongruous place for a beat scene but due to its sense of its own propriety, the town tolerated many eccentrics during the late fifties, little suspecting they would be the forerunners of the hippies in the sixties. *38 Priory Street and All That Jazz*, a short book written by John Appleby, describes Vladimir Levinski, a local character and a Cheltenham musician, who was outrageous even by today's standards:

HIS CLOTHES LIKE HIS VIEWS WERE distinctly Edwardian in character. Regardless of the weather, even on summer's hottest day, Vladimir emerged dressed in a long woolen overcoat. He wore jackboots and sported a monocle to go with an almost permanent Manikin cigar. . . . In those days long hair was hardly a masculine fashion, so that as Vladimir's flowing, curly ginger crop fanned outwards as well as downwards, it drew curious stares from those passing through the town. Residents knew better than to glance, for they knew that Vladimir could out-stare any of them, sitting on his Promenade seat . . . and making noises of disapproval.

As a pianist, audiences found him both brilliant and temperamental. There was the occasion when he "took" the Cheltenham Town Hall one night and proceeded to give a magnificent performance. But, for some reason better known to himself, he was displeased and strode off the stage halfway through the concert, throwing sheets of music about him as he left.

Hanging out at the El Flam, Brian became friendly with John Appleby, ten years his senior and a kind, approachable man. John was the only one of Brian's friends who maintained a relationship with both Brian and his parents. After Brian's death, Lewis Jones wrote John a letter thanking him for the friendship he had given Brian, and although Brian was gone, Lewis hoped that John would visit him and Mrs. Jones. The friendship had begun one night in 1960, when John Appleby picked up Brian at his parents' house for a party. Mrs. Jones met John at the door and hurried him into the living room: "John, I must have a word with you about Brian. We're quite worried because he's running around too much. He's in and out of the Waikiki and The Bar-B-Que and all the rest and he goes to parties every night. He doesn't seem the least inclined to do any work. Please see what you can do about it." The next moment they heard a rush down the stairs and the living room door was thrown open by Brian.

As Brian and John drove off Mrs. Jones winked at John. John said, "Brian, I want to have a word with you. . . . Now then, it's about time you got a job, isn't it?"

"Don't you start . . ." Brian commanded good-naturedly.

John continued, "Well, I am starting; now you've got to do something about it. Look, the Cheltenham District Transfer Co. are very short of bus conductors. I'm suggesting you go down tomorrow and see Mr. Hannis about a temporary job."

"Oh, I'm not going."

"Look, Brian, if you don't go I am coming around tomorrow morning and dragging you out of bed and pushing you into Ken Hannis's office."

"Oh, all right, if you insist. I'm not going to be taken there. I'm old enough to look after myself."

The next evening John received a very humble phone call: "Oh John, Brian here. You'd be interested to know I'm starting the job on Monday."

Brian became a conductor on the double-decker buses. He enjoyed the job and reported to John that he was surprised by the things that happen on buses and the different kinds of people he met. John knew the driver for Brian's bus who later told John, "This young friend of yours is almost bringing bus service to a standstill. He finds it difficult to get up." Brian lasted at the job for three weeks.

Brian found a father-substitute in John Appleby. John's great love in life has always been British trams. He zealously participated in the Tramway Museum Society which was dedicated to restoring old trams. Although Brian occasionally worked with John on the trams, he was more interested in being with John than the work itself. To Brian these Sunday outings were laced with the warm intimacy that a boy can share with his father.

Years later, when Brian was a successful Rolling Stone, he returned to Cheltenham and visited old haunts with John. As soon as Brian arrived in town he phoned John, "Will you please come round and pick me up . . . and by the way, do you still have that 1752 FH (John's old Vauxhall car's registration)?" John said that he did.

"Thank God something in this world doesn't change," Brian said. As if to say, life was better in some ways before he became a famous Rolling Stone.

When Brian and John arrived at a local pub, people would crowd around for his autograph. One young man asked John what it was like to be a pop star's father. John replied, "Actually, I'm not his father. . . ." Brian spun around, grinning all over: "John's my second father." Even Lewis Jones acknowledged, on more than one occasion, that John knew Brian better than he did.

In 1961, Pat Andrews, an attractive brunette with a teased bouffant hairstyle, noticed Brian around town. He always seemed to be on his own, a loner standing off on the side quietly watching the action. She thought Brian, with his shaggy blond hair was the scruffiest person she had ever seen, yet he intrigued her and she wanted to meet him. At a matinee one Sunday, a mutual friend (who was at the movie with Brian) introduced them. Brian took Pat out for coffee, walked her home and asked her out. Pat explained in an interview five years later why she went out with Brian: "I was sorry for him because he seemed so lonely and I was curious to find out why people wouldn't talk to him."

Since Brian's parents were nagging him to get a job, he found work on a coal delivery truck. Knowing that his parents would feel that this job was not appropriate for an ex-pupil of the Cheltenham Grammar School, Brian decided not to tell them. Instead, he changed clothes and showered at a friend's house after work and told his parents he had a more respectable job. With his first paycheck, he bought Pat two necklaces as a birthday present. Too impatient to take time to shower, he picked her up at work. He was covered in coal dust. They couldn't go out unless he changed, so Brian decided to go home and face his parents. Unfortunately, he had forgotten that his parents were away on a short trip and had locked up the house. Pat and Brian broke in and Brian changed his clothes, but in the meantime a neighbor had seen them and called the police. Brian then decided to move into a spare room in Pat's married sister's apartment.

Brian and Pat had begun sleeping together. Brian still felt jealous and threatened by Pat's male friends, although everyone who knew the couple agreed that Pat was devoted to Brian. Once, when Brian found a letter from one of Pat's old boyfriends, he ripped it up in front of all their friends in a coffee bar. He wanted Pat's complete attention and his freedom at the same time.

The couple were soon seeing each other every night. They went to rehearsals of a local group, the Cheltone Six. The popular music at the time was traditional jazz. Brian loved music and seemed happiest when tinkering with a guitar. Brian had gotten his first guitar, a Spanish model, for three pounds. It was almost impossible to get a recognizable melody out of it. Brian soon realized that he preferred to play rhythm 'n' blues, with its various tempos and meaningful lyrics, than traditional jazz.

For Brian Jones, music was obviously a way out of his middle-class situation. Rock 'n' Roll was a path to riches and bohemian freedom. It was also a way to distinguish yourself from the mainstream, to be special. Rock 'n' roll offered the chance for power, freedom, sex, and money to a pretty young boy. As Simon Frith said in his brilliant analysis of youth and leisure, *Sound Effects*, "Bohemian freedom, particularly in its young rebel version, is defined primarily against the family. It is from their families that the young must escape, it is through their family quarrels that they must first recognize themselves as rebels, and it is their refusal to settle down to a respectable domestic life that makes their rebellion permanent."

In Peter Wilmott's book, *Adolescent Boys of East-London* the boy he described could almost be a young Brian Jones: "He was alone, playing records by Billie Holiday and Miles Davis. He says of his parents, 'They couldn't understand me in a hundred years. Like most ordinary East End people, their idea of living is to have a steady job and settle down with a nice little wife in a nice little house or flat, doing the same things every day of your life. They think the sort of things I do are mad.' What sort of things? 'Well, I might decide to take the day off and go up to a park and sit and meditate. Or go round my friend's pad for an all-night session. A group of us drink whiskey and smoke tea and talk about what's happiness and things like that.'"

Brian sought out others with whom he could share his love of the blues. This was a difficult search since most people listened to traditional jazz. But when Kenny Ball's band played the Cheltenham Rotunda, Brian met Richard Hattrell, whom he had seen at many local band performances. Brian went right up to Richard, introduced himself, and asked Richard to help him find any available Muddy Waters records. The next day Richard scoured his mounds of blues catalogues and compiled an extensive list for Brian. Brian was delighted to find someone, at last, who spoke his language. Brian talked to Richard about music for endless hours; together they saw every band that played in the area.

Richard loved rhythm 'n' blues. He was carried away by the blues at a very young age and never abandoned it. Jack Bruce (the bass player in Cream), with whom he studied bass, found him "very promising." And although Hattrell has worked over the years as a barman near Cheltenham, he has maintained friendships with many British rock musicians.

Richard valued Brian more as a musician than as an interesting friend. He felt Brian's death was a great loss because he was an important musical talent. (Hattrell instantly assumed that this author was writing Brian's biography in tribute to Brian's musical skills.)

More essential, however, was Brian's realization that Richard's non-threatening attitude was even more important than his interest in the blues. Richard, devoted to the God-like mystique of musically gifted people, would not intimidate Brian.

Brian's and Richard's fathers found their sons' wild lives intolerable. They insisted that if Richard and Brian continued to stay up late and party and hang-out in coffee bars, they would have to live elsewhere. (Although Brian had moved in with Pat's sister after breaking into his parent's house, he had returned home a few days later.) The boys moved in with some local art students. The move was significant to Brian because he felt he could never go back. Richard remained close to his family, returning home for lunch every Sunday. He often brought Brian along, yet Richard never visited Brian's house and never met Brian's parents. Brian would often say that he didn't like his parents at all and felt they had rejected him. Brian frequently told friends that he wished his house resembled the Hattrells'. Although Mr. Hattrell, a solicitor (lawyer) and an ex-British Army colonel, disapproved of Brian and Richard's lifestyle, he was still able to talk with them.

Unable to totally divorce himself from his parents' expectations, Brian next worked as a junior architect with the Cheltenham Council, but he was still bent on exorcising his Cheltenham upbringing. Brian and Richard rented an apartment across town on Pressbury Road. Like New Orleans musicians, they organized "rent parties." The two provided the food, liquor, and atmosphere, and guests paid a small amount at the door. Any profit, including returned bottles, paid the rent. Blues notables such as Sonny Boy Williamson, Muddy Waters, and Howlin' Wolf, who often toured England with Chris Barber's traditional Jazz Band frequented the parties and played for free. Any band playing nearby would drop in after a gig. Party regulars were Eric Annenball's Dixieland Knights. The Knights might have been playing anywhere within a fifty-mile radius and when they were already wound-up after a gig, they would come to the party and blow all night. Once when Richard was working at an electrical shop, the Knights paraded him from his apartment to the shop all the way across town at 8:00 A.M.—as staid Cheltenhamians stared aghast. At parties, Brian also began drinking whiskey in moderation to loosen up.

Music dominated most of Brian's time. He had quit his job at the architect's office because it reminded him of his background, the very situation he was fleeing. His next job, selling records, fit more closely the image he wanted to create. The record shop exposed him to different kinds of music. Since Richard was also immersed in music, little else diverted them. If Brian was not playing guitar, he was listening to his records, his only valued possessions.

Pat Andrews visited the apartment regularly, often cooking dinner for the boys. By now, she was pregnant by

Brian and wanted to have the baby. He wanted to have the baby adopted. His new independent life excited him and he felt torn. Pat had been convenient. On payday Brian waited for her outside the chemist shop where she worked and took her wages; she never argued. He used her money to pay the rent and buy new guitar strings. Brian was growing tired of Pat even before she was pregnant, but suddenly he felt trapped and burdened by the whole situation. When visiting her relatives in London, they would go to numerous jazz clubs. Brian talked to the artists and Pat sulked in the corner. Trying to avoid the nagging reality of fatherhood, Brian saw other women when Pat was too pregnant to go out.

Pat had been defying her parents, who begged her not to see Brian, when she learned that Brian was seeing other women. The couple argued about Brian's infidelity and to make peace, he promised to be faithful. When Pat entered the hospital in October 1961, she worried that Brian would not even visit her. That afternoon, a gigantic bunch of flowers walked toward her; behind them was Brian. He had sold his records to pay for the flowers. Pat cried. (Brian's records were his most precious possessions.)

Brian was proud of the baby. He named him Julian after his favorite jazz musician, Julian "Cannonball" Adderley. Pat and the baby lived at Pat's house while Brian continued to live with Richard. Brian again changed jobs, and he bought the baby a rattle and Pat a handbag, skirt, sweater, and umbrella with his first paycheck.

At home, Brian practiced on his cheap guitar, using a converted tape recorder as amplifier. He taught himself to play the slide guitar from listening to Elmore James records. Elmore was one of his idols and Brian even used "Elmore Jones" as his stage name.

Brian began to play with a Cheltenham jazz band. After the sets girls would hang around the band, flirting with

Brian, and Pat's jealousy soared to new heights. They argued frequently, and during one fight, Brian blackened Pat's eye and she ran home. Three hours later Pat heard a tapping noise at her window. Brian was throwing pebbles at the window and wanted to apologize.

Another of Brian's idols was Johnny Cash, the only country musician he liked and the only lyricist he studied; every phrase and nuance meant something special. Cash's music relaxed Brian and he would fall asleep listening to a stack of records. When he woke up, he used the first song he thought of as a guide; if he remembered a traveling song, Richard and he would hitch down to London and listen to music. Brian venerated Cash's romantic image of the successful loner, a man who's tried just about everything and survived.

Another of Brian and Richard's musical idols was Alexis Korner. They taped his music off the radio, and played it back so many times that the tape practically fell apart. Alexis's guitar playing, in turn, was influenced by Muddy Waters. This was the music Brian wanted to play.

Late in 1960, Chris Barber's Jazz Band was promoting rhythm 'n' blues in Britain, and Barber brought a Chicago harmonica player, Sonny Boy Williamson, to Cheltenham. The next year he brought Alexis Korner with him. The Cheltenham Town Hall housed a capacity crowd, even though only two people out of a thousand felt fanatically about Alexis. Chris Barber announced, "Now I'd like to introduce to you the man I consider to be the finest exponent of the blues in this country . . . Alexis Korner." "Yeahhhhhhhh!" Brian and Richard screamed. They sat in the balcony and jumped about with sheer joy. The other 998 people looked at them as if to say, "What the hell's going on?"

After the gig, Brian and Richard went backstage. Alexis told them, "It's really a pleasure to meet two people in

Cheltenham who are so into the blues and, moreover, have heard of me. I'm starting a new blues band. We'll be playing at the Ealing Broadway Club in London beginning on St. Patrick's Day. Why don't you come down?''

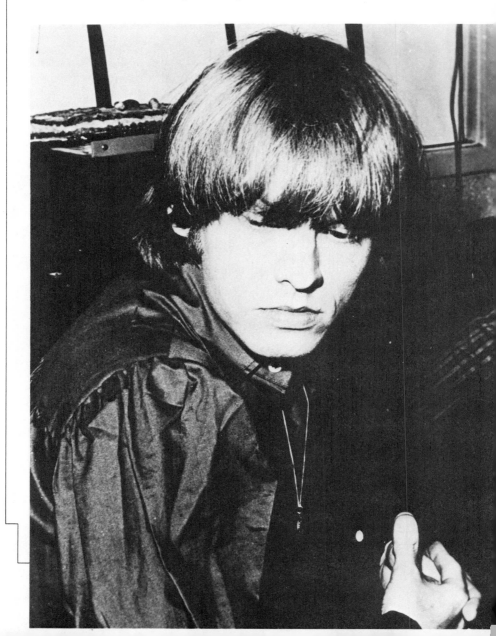

II

Alexis Korner and Cyril Davies were founders of the Ealing Jazz Club. None of the traditional London jazz clubs would let them play electric music, so on St. Patrick's Day, 1962, they opened their own club in a suburb of London. They put up a handful of posters, hoping to attract a small crowd. By the second Saturday, people from as far away as Scotland packed the club.

Brian and Richard hitchhiked down from Cheltenham. "The hours and hours of hitching we did were worth it." Richard said, "The club was located dead opposite the Ealing Broadway tube station. It was the first rhythm 'n' blues club, not just in London, but in all of Europe. Cyril Davies, Johnny Parker, a pianist who now plays for Kenny Ball's band, Jack Bruce, Dick Heckstall-Smith, tenor saxophonist, and singer John Baldry made up Alexis' band." Soon, people from all over Europe congregated there: future rock stars Keith Relf, Eric Clapton, the Rolling Stones, jazz musicians and music journalists.

"It was a fantastic scene," Hattrell remembered. "We would get so wound up, it was incredible. We were spaced out, literally, with music. We had a good drink as well, but it was the music that excited us so much. We would get back on the tube and there would be eight hundred people singin' that Muddy Waters song 'Hootchie Cootchie Man.' The whole flippin' tube was rockin' like mad."

On many weekends Brian and Richard would camp out on Alexis' floor and talk about blues until dawn. Brian did mention to Alexis that he could not stand Cheltenham but did not supply many details. "No one really knew very much about Brian's home life," Alexis said, "because he was very careful not to involve his escape route—music—with the middle-class past he was escaping from."

Whenever he could afford it, Brian hitched to London, and that city gradually became the center of his life. While the security of Cheltenham was still enticing, the clubs, the music, and the looseness of London proved irresistible until, finally, he packed a suitcase and moved there to stay.

Brian's move depressed Pat. His daily letters did not make up for the rumors that he was seeing other women. On Easter Sunday in 1962, with one pound in her pocket, she took the 3:00 A.M. bus to London and arrived at Brian's door with a suitcase and the baby. Pat banged on the door. Brian, in his pajamas, answered, and he was alone. Together, they moved to a bedsitter (a combination bedroom-sitting room apartment) with a kitchenette and found jobs: Pat in a laundry, Brian in a department store. Between them they earned the equivalent of forty dollars a week.

But the couple still fought. "Brian didn't want to be with her," Richard Hattrell said. "He wanted the high lights and beautiful girls who made eyes at him while he was performing. Pat was a very ordinary girl; not at all artistic. She didn't really appreciate music. Pat was convenient; someone to clean the flat, cook his food, and provide a sexual outlet."

Brian placed an ad in *Jazz News* magazine soliciting musicians to form a rhythm and blues group. Ian "Stew" Stewart, piano player, answered Brian's ad. Stew, who has been with the Rolling Stones longer than anyone, first as an on-stage member and later as road manager, described Brian's apartment: "He was livin' in an unbelievable awful state; drinkin' spaghetti out of a cup. I thought it was a stunt! But they had no money whatsoever. We talked about music and Brian said that he was gonna have a rehearsal Monday.

"The rehearsal consisted of another piano player, a singer, Andy Wren, and Brian on regular and slide guitar. Brian was very functional. We rehearsed a couple of times. Sometimes guitarist Jeff Bradford joined us—very good, but a great purist. He wouldn't bend at all."

Brian and Richard were regulars at the Ealing Jazz Club, and Alexis would encourage musicians to sit in with the band. "Brian was dying to play," Richard said. "He was really a good guitar player, even on that homemade amplifier of his. You could tell that the sounds were there. He played slide guitar before the average British guitarist had heard of it.

"Keith Richard and Mick Jagger also hung out at the Ealing. Brian sat in playing guitar. Sometimes Keith sang the blues. Mick sang and was learning the harmonica. Brian played professional standard harmonica long before Mick did; Mick got everything from Brian's harmonica playing. All of us got friendly because we loved the music. There was only a small nucleus of us in London who were really into the blues. Other people went to the Ealing because of the lively atmosphere."

The first time Keith Richard heard Brian play slide guitar, he was greatly impressed. "Brian was the first person I heard playing the slide electric guitar," he recalled. "He played with Alexis one night at the Ealing Club. Mick and I both thought he was incredible. Mick went up to talk to him for a bit. That's when Brian mentioned he was forming a band."

Many musicians, including Jack Bruce, Eric Clapton, and Manfred Mann, congregated at the Ealing. Brian could have easily joined another group. But as Richard emphasized, "He wanted to form his own group. The Rolling Stones was Brian's baby."

Joining another band would never do for Brian. He had to create the band himself. He needed to be the leader—the most powerful and pivotal member. To be part of something else would have defeated one of Brian's major reasons for playing music. He wanted to see his own vision shaped and reflected. This was one reason why it was impossible to be *just* a Rolling Stone. When Brian was no longer the leader, his motivation was destroyed. Being the leader was as important, perhaps even more, as playing music.

Brian continued to rehearse his band with Ian, Andy, and Jeff, but they couldn't scrounge up any club dates. Mick came to some rehearsals but wouldn't join the group unless Keith was included. Since they needed a bass player, Keith's friend Dick Taylor filled the position. They rehearsed on and off for the next year, sometimes not seeing each other for a few months. But the group was shaping up and Brian was in charge.

Keith described Brian at that point: "He was in the process of getting a band together and moving up to London with one of his many women [Pat] and children. God knows how many he had. . . . He was a good guitar player then. He had the touch and was just peaking . . . he was really working at it. We said, 'We're just amateurs, but we dig to play.' He invited me up to listen to what he was getting together in some pub in London . . . that's where I met Stew. He was with Brian."

During this time, Brian continued to live with Pat. The relationship went from bad to worse. Brian spent all his money on guitar strings and records, while Pat paid for their food (which often consisted of cucumber sandwiches). "One afternoon," Keith recalled, "Mick went round to their flat to see Brian. He wasn't in and Mick knocked off his old lady. It became an incredible triangle." Eventually, after Brian was fired from his job for stealing some money, Pat returned to Cheltenham. This incident may have marked the beginning of the competition between Mick and Brian.

Brian, Mick, and Keith rented a dingy apartment together on Edith Grove in Chelsea, and Richard Hattrell soon joined them. Mick had a university grant and went to his classes. Brian procured odd jobs from time to time, but Keith, who received a small allowance from his family, never worked. Brian and Keith used to practice guitar until, without either of them as yet being outstanding solo players, they played extremely well as a team.

Keith was Brian's first close male friend. Although he was very friendly with Hattrell and Appleby, they did not provide the warm, good-time relationship he found with Keith. "Of Brian, Mick, and Keith, Keith is the most open," Alexis said. "Keith is the least interested in portraying himself as something other than what he is. Brian was interested in presenting himself as any of the fantasies he had of himself. Mick has always been very deliberate about the way he presents himself."

The friendship with Keith meant a great deal to Brian. Keith was devoid of the anxieties that Brian tried to keep at bay. Keith was cool. He didn't gum things up by worrying. Keith enjoyed his life and usually felt assured that life wouldn't wash him over. Brian wanted that ease too; he was tired of treading water.

At this point, Mick was still tied to the London School of Economics. Brian and Keith's friendship blossomed. Some of those close to the Rolling Stones have thought that the balance of power within the band shifts with whomever has Keith's affection and allegiance. "There was always this incredible three-way conflict between Brian, Mick, and myself," Keith said, "where it was imbalanced in one way or another. It was either Brian and I, and Mick with a different point of view. Or later on, Mick and I together, which made Brian very bitter at one point. It started out with Brian and I being more friendly because we were completely dedicated to the idea of getting this band together. Brian and I were hanging around all day doing nothing—avoiding paying the rent, trying to find food. Whereas Mick was taking it as a sideline thing. You would only see Mick occasionally, coming in the evening. Anyway he had much more of a serious thing going. He was a student at LSE and as far as he was concerned that's where he was headed. It wasn't until it became apparent that there was something there that Mick could put more of his energies into it, began to take it more seriously. It was really a big thing for Mick to give school up, whereas Brian and I had absolutely nothing to lose."

"We used to sit around and play guitar together all the time, just to keep warm. It was the cheapest way. And that went on for ages. For the first six months all the Rolling Stones did was rehearse. They never actually played a gig. They just rehearsed and rehearsed."

Sometimes they performed at clubs around London. Brian had named the group "Rollin' Stones" after a Muddy Waters song, "Rollin' Stone Blues." Richard Hattrell, acting as road manager, mapped out routes via the subway stops. The band spent more money traveling to gigs than they received for playing. The would either take the bus or the subway as the other passengers gaped in amazement at all the equipment.

As Brian grew tighter with Mick and Keith, his relationship with Richard became more difficult to maintain. Alexis, who still maintains a friendship with Richard, said, "Because of Brian's particular insecurity, he was very heavy on anyone else's insecurity. Obviously, I dug Brian, but he could be very mean. Just plain evil, like twisting words and finding a way of saying something that would hurt without it sounding like that at the time. Or he used his face very much for expression. He had a very mobile face to start out with anyway. Brian made sure that if he was being ironic—even if the words sounded strange—you knew. Like digging the thing in. And he did it with Richard. He did it with anyone who would let him."

Keith related an unforgettable incident between Brian and Richard Hattrell: "Dick Hattrell was in this territorial army thing—two weeks summer camp. Then he'd come to London, meet Brian and rave it up. They'd go down to all the jazz clubs and I think they'd done this for a couple of years before I knew Brian. And this particular September or October '62, Brian was just in London to form the Stones. He had just gotten together with Ian Stewart. Mick Jagger [was] diggin' it very much, working with Alexis and getting more money for doing his high society jobs, which Alexis used to come by. Mick used to dig the deb scene. This was the first year that Brian had his group there and started rehearsing it. And Dick Hattrell came to town with his eighty quid in his grey top pocket. Of course the first time, instead of being incredibly nice to Dick, as Brian usually was when there's nothing to interfere with the relationship, he was hanging out with me and Mick and the rest of the Stones. Obviously, he didn't want us to think of his association with Dick Hattrell too seriously—too provincial a thing. He didn't want to be thought of as being part of some hick country scene. And Dick was like a complete puppy toward Brian. At that time Brian was incredible. Within two weeks the eighty pounds was gone, and he had conned Dick into buying him this new electric guitar.

"Brian, Dick, and me would walk to Wimpy Bars to eat and Brian would make Dick walk ten yards behind. Brian would invite Dick to lunch and the three of us would go to what we considered then a really good restaurant and have a hot meal—which nobody could afford, of course. Then we'd just walk out and leave Dick Hattrell with the bill. Did the usual things until the poor cat had nothing except his overcoat.

"And then Brian pulled this incredible stroke. Brian and I were so crazy at the time and did mad things. (We were living at Edith Grove in Chelsea.) Anyway, Brian had these two absolutely harmless wires that were plugged into the back of some inert piece of machinery. Brian had threatened to electrocute him, chasing him around the room with these two wires. And Dick Hattrell was petrified. He eventually made Dick sit outside on the front steps half the night and it snowed, a very early snow. The poor guy actually did what he was told 'cause Brian had said 'Stay out on the doorstep or else I'll give you 220 volts.' And people'd be coming in and out and they'd say, 'Man, there's this guy on your doorstep absolutely shivering.' And Brian let him in four hours later. The poor guy completely freaked out.

"And other times he'd be incredibly nice to Dick. Later on Brian helped him. I vaguely heard that he'd been to visit Dick. Hattrell used to come to our gigs later on when we were playing in the area. I think as long as none of the Stones were around them, Brian was probably very nice to him."

Dick Hattrell attributed Brian's cruelty to an artistic temperament: "He had an artistic way in his life. You know how an artist can be elated one moment, down the next? With Brian it was more. One minute he'd really be raving, not literally screaming his head off, but really excited, like the first time Alexis played the town hall. The next thing he could be really down. I shall never forget one occasion when we were all living at Edith Grove, in Chelsea. It was snowing and all the rest and he sent me out for some fags, and he locked me out for the rest of the night. Just didn't want me to come back in at that particular time. He had a cruel steak in him. He felt the lull. He always wanted something new to be happening, so when there wasn't any excitement he was trying to find new ways of excitement."

Brian dominated people by capitalizing on their insecurities. This tactic gave him control and power, but was

Brian shortly after the first American tour of the Rolling Stones. August 1964.

not fulfilling or even a real release for the pent-up emotions he was distorting. "He didn't know how to deal with people anyway," Giorgio Gomelsky, first promoter of the Rolling Stones, said. "He could only deal with people if he either frightened them or if he dominated them, which is the same. And fear and a dark kind of humor. He was very cruel. Almost to spite himself, you knew he wished he wasn't doing it—what he was doing. He couldn't stop himself."

Kathy Etchingham, a woman who lived with Jimi Hendrix for two years and had a platonic friendship with Brian, related how he treated the women he casually slept with during 1967 to 1969: "He did some bloody evil things to me. We went to this party together and he told me that the drinks were in the garage. So I went marching back there. What he didn't tell me was there was a big hole in the floor and I went straight into it. He thought it was very very funny. I have no skin on my knees and elbows and he was behind me when I walked in and had brought a few friends to watch . . . .

"Sometimes when there was a chick there he used to talk about our sex life together and we didn't even have one. That's how he used to get rid of them. Anytime he wanted to get rid of a chick he would just call me up. Once he chased me around his flat telling the chick that was there that I liked bottles. He would never tell them that he was inviting someone else over. He would just go upstairs and go to a phone and say to me, 'Come over, we'll have a laugh.' I just used to show up and the chick would say, 'Who is this?' He had this impish smile."

"Sometimes when I would go upstairs to the bathroom, he would come upstairs and we would sit in his bedroom and talk for a half an hour and leave them downstairs alone. Sometimes there would be two or three chicks because Brian often liked more than one at a time, and he would walk back downstairs and say, 'It's about time you left isn't it.' They were just starfuckers. One time I went over there after he called and he was in bed with two chicks. He just threw their clothes on the bed and said, [to them], 'Do you mind leaving?' "

The Stones continued practicing without much outside interest in the band. Brian suddenly grew panicky that perhaps he had made the wrong decision. In Pete Goodman's book, *Our Own Story*, on the Rolling Stones, Brian said of this particular time: "I remember one chat between the three of us, with a Muddy Waters long player providing the background music. . . . We wondered if we were doing the right thing by not getting into worthwhile jobs and forgetting all about this music bit. . . . Suppose we failed. Suppose we went on not doing much, just soaking up music, for a whole year. That would be the limit, we reckoned. If we flopped—would it matter? At least we'd have tried . . . ."

Keith and Brian thought that the Stones' future looked bleak, and maybe the two should try to make it as a duo. "There was this point in '62," Keith said, "that Brian and I had decided that this rhythm 'n' blues thing was absolutely a flop. We weren't gonna get away with it. Brian and I were gonna do an Everly Brothers thing, so we spent three or four days in the kitchen rehearsing these terrible songs. Then we decided we'd write a song too. The song sounded like a 1920's Broadway musical—just the weirdest kind of song. Brian was utterly impossible to write a song with. *He* wrote the song because he would dominate anything he was into; there was no way you could suggest anything. But then Brian wouldn't make a decision about chord changes, where the changes should go. And then he said that Mick had to sing it. Mick just couldn't get around it. At that time, Mick could only sing a twelve-bar blues."

Brian and Keith came from different educational backgrounds. Brian, from middle-class Cheltenham, had been programmed for intellectual achievement. Keith, from a working-class family, had no such leanings. He attended Sidcup Art School, just outside of London. Sidcup's atmosphere was infinitely looser than that of Cheltenham's Promenade. Many rock stars came from art schools—John Lennon and David Bowie, for example. "I did graphic design and life drawing for three years," Keith said. "But basically, I played guitar. I got my first guitar when I was fifteen and just beginning art school. There were a lot of other guitar players in art school. From this particular scene we've got myself, Mick, and Dick Taylor, who'd known each other. Dick Taylor, who went to my art school, was playing with us for a while. He went to play with the Pretty Things, along with Phil May, who also came from Sidcup. It's a funny sort of breeding ground."

Alexis attributed Brian's song-writing difficulties to Brian's tendency to conclude a task in his head before he ever really embarked on it: "Brian had a problem which quite a lot of us have—who have suffered or benefited from a certain amount of education (whichever point of view you wish to adopt)—you have this awful habit of thinking something out before you've done it, so that the actual doing is totally unsatisfactory. The task has been accomplished—finished before you've started—and that's an enormous frustration. And that was Brian's great frustration: the amount of education he had and the way he thought. He thought very fast, not always very straight, but very fast and very hard. And he would conclude an entire episode before he even started it."

Keith and Brian shared their obsession: "I found myself very much with Brian," Keith said, "playing music, listening to records over and over again trying to figure it all out, how it's actually played, for hours and hours every day. At this point Brian was a phenomenal guitarist. He always had to work at it because he never did develop a style particularly of his own. He used to get turned on by listening.

"At the point where Mick and I met Brian, Brian's version of the blues was Muddy Waters, Elmore James, Sonny Boy Williamson, Howlin' Wolf, and John Lee Hooker. Whereas Mick and I were pushing people apart from Muddy Waters. Obviously I wanted that, but we were also very much more into Chuck Berry, Jimmy Reed, Bo Diddley. And Brian never heard of Chuck Berry. He didn't consider Chuck Berry to be in the same class or area, but when we proved to him that he was, then he really started to dig him. He sort of discarded his old Elmore James things."

"I think the first one he got into was Jimmy Reed. Brian would sit around for hours and hours and hours working out how Jimmy Reed's sound was put together. He'd work at it and work at it. He'd really get it down. He was a very good guitar player at that point for what he was doing."

"After that he'd work with me on some of the Chuck Berry style things. We really got into that. We were working out the guitar parts and actually the rhythm that the people were playing was a 4/4 swing beat, not at all a rock beat. It was a jazz swing beat, except there would be another guitar playing."

Through listening to Jimmy Reed records and hanging out with Cyril Davies, Brian began to experiment with the harmonica. Brian imitated Reed's lazy style and practiced Davies' technique of bending and flattening the notes. Brian visited Cyril at home and the two would blow harmonica together. In a few years Brian would find the limitations of the guitar boring and he searched for musical stimulation from more exotic sounds. The harmonica was the first step in this musical departure.

In the early fifties, modern jazz was popular in England. Then rock 'n' roll flourished with American stars like Little Richard, Bill Haley, and Elvis. By 1960, the first excitement had worn itself out. People were playing a watered-down sort of pop music. It had little relation to its origins. It was time for a change, and London was ripe for something big. The blues revival began.

Keith sized up the situation: "What we did, along with Alexis, was to take over the traditional jazz circuit. And, within a period of six to nine months, we put all of those jazz bands out of work. Traditional jazz had been a huge fad in England for two or three years, especially among the art students and people who couldn't get into that pop stuff that was around. It was at a point where rock 'n' roll had gotten very watered down. Fifties rock 'n' roll had come and passed already. That's what we were trying to play in '61 and '62 and nobody wanted to hear it because it was old hat by then. It was all over. So we couldn't call ourselves a rock 'n' roll band 'cause it was already out of date. But we were so much more heavily influenced by blues people than just rock 'n' roll people. Although in America the division was not so obvious because there were records that had been coming out, especially from the ghettos, since the end of the war with that beat—with that feel. In England, that beat was something nobody heard until *Blackboard Jungle* and 'Rock Around the Clock' ten years later."

The Stones got their first big break on July 12, 1962 when they stood in for Alexis' band at the Marquee Club, in London. By now, the Stones and Alexis had built up a tremendous following in London's West End. The crowds at Alexis' Saturday night show had grown so big that the owners of the Marquee Club, John Gee and Harold Pendleton, asked Alexis to play on Thursday night as well. BBC radio then signed him to do a jazz program. When Alexis asked Brian, Keith, and company if they would like to do his Marquee Club gig, they were ecstatic. The line-up, according to *Jazz News,* was Brian on lead guitar, Mick on vocals, Keith on rhythm guitar, Dick Taylor on bass, Ian Stewart on piano, and Mike Avery on drums. Charlie Watts was the drummer in Alexis' band and Taylor, who soon left the fledgling band when he was accepted at the Royal College of Art, was later replaced by Bill Wyman. Mike Avery is the drummer for the Kinks.

The Marquee gig was a success. Brian began promoting the band. He made friends with journalists and club owners. In retrospect, these months were the most successful and happiest of Brian's life. He felt exhilarated and knew that he was accomplishing something. Members of the band were even talking offhand about removing Mick as lead singer. Brian wanted Paul Jones, later the lead vocalist for Manfred Mann, to sing. Paul Jones had been singing with Alexis Korner. They wanted to keep Mick in the group, but find someone else who could sing better. One night, during rehearsal, the boys were overhead saying, "Oh, Mick, you're so bad . . . but you're doing great!" They thought it was great the way Mick shook his head around.

The Stones' popularity was growing. Fans would hitch to the gigs from miles around, just as Brian had, to hear Alexis at the Ealing Jazz Club. In the beginning about twenty people showed up to see them play, but within months, through word-of-mouth reputation, hundreds of people were crowding in. The next step was a recording session.

The senior engineer at I.B.C. Recording Studio, Glyn Johns, who later worked with the Beatles, ran a pub in Surrey called the Red Lion. He and his partner managed the pub on alternate weeks. During one of Glyn's alternate weeks, the Stones played there. Glyn saw their act, and was impressed enough by their music to take them to I.B.C. Studio to record five cuts. The Stones were not yet signed to a label, and the tapes were never released. "They were novel," Glyn said, "because nobody had every heard of Jimmy Reed and Bo Diddley and that was basically what they were doing."

At the recording session, Brian directed the group. "Brian was pretty much the leader," Glyn said. "He was certainly the spokesman for the group to me. This was their first recording session and Brian was very much concerned about the sounds that I would produce on tape. He had an exact rhythm 'n' blues sound he wanted: the Jimmy Reed-type sound, which was virtually unheard of in England. It wasn't just the music that was unusual, but the actual recorded sound was completely different than normal rock 'n' roll. Fortunately, I'd been into Jimmy Reed for some time and very much into his sound as well."

On those first tracks, Brian played harmonica, guitar, and sang backup. The tracks were "Diddley Daddy," "Road Runner," "Bright Lights, Big City," "I Want to be Loved," and "Honey, What's Wrong?" He presented himself to Glyn as someone who wanted to be respected as a musician. Brian had often stated that he thought singers were inferior musicians. Only a musician could gain his respect. Hattrell said, "Brian sang a bit of backup, but he put singers down. Singers weren't musicians and Brian had strong feelings about this: somebody who plays an instrument is somebody to be respected. Anybody can sing."

These were reportedly Brian's favorite tracks. He was more proud of them than anything else the Rolling Stones ever recorded. He would play these songs over and over for visitors, as if to say: "this is what I wanted; this is what we used to be. . . ."

Enter Giorgio Gomelsky, an integral part of the budding musical scene, who had been involved in music ever since he was twelve and turned on to Charlie Parker. In 1962, he was making documentary films about music. He was responsible for bringing Sonny Boy Williamson to Liverpool to take part in one of his blues events.

Giorgio remembered that in 1962 and '63: "Up in Liverpool, it was really happening. Down in London, nobody knew anything about it. Brian Epstein had just come to manage the Beatles. He didn't know much about management. He kept on saying, 'I don't know. I don't know,' and people kept doubling their prices. People would call him up and say, 'Are your boys free on the 17th of October?'

" 'Yes . . .Well . . . I don't know.'

" 'I'll give you a hundred pounds.'

" 'Well . . . I don't know.' He was looking for the date-sheet and kept saying, 'I don't know' because he didn't know if the Beatles were free. The other guy thought, 'I don't know' was because of the money. So Brian Epstein ended up doing five-hundred pound gigs that started out for fifty quid."

The atmosphere in England was building with pockets of rock 'n' roll spilling over and flooding London. "There were these separate areas," Donovan explained, "St. Albans, Cheltenham, Liverpool, that were making their statement. But then a few of them crashed through into popularity. . . .The whole movement was so exciting because it was localized everywhere." During this period, you could wander into a club in Hamburg, Germany and see a rock 'n' roll band headed by a guy named Tony Sheridan. You could hang out at their jam sessions until six in the morning only to find out, after months, that they were the Beatles.

During 1963, Giorgio ran a club in Richmond called the Station Hotel. One evening the regular band didn't show up. Giorgio had previously told Brian that if there ever was an opening for the Rolling Stones, he would contact him—and he did. "A revolution in the taste of music had to happen," Giorgio said, "and I was helping. Brian was the energy in the band. He felt what he wanted to do. He was the only one who knew."

Some people consider the booking at the Station Hotel as the Rolling Stones' "big break." The significant aspect was that Giorgio managed to get Peter Jones, an important pop journalist, down to the club to hear the Stones. "Giorgio Gomelsky was making a film," Peter Jones said, "which he hoped would represent British rhythm 'n' blues. He found this band which, to him, was doing very well. He was also tending to promote them in the pub down there. He started filming and *demanded* that I come and see them this Sunday morning. I really wasn't very keen 'cause you hear this every other day: there's always something big coming.

"Anyway, they were really very good. Two of them came out during the lunch break: Mick and Brian. And one thing that I'm absolutely certain about: there was no doubt that Brian really was the leader of the band. Brian was the one who knew precisely what they were doing. He was the organizing one. He had this great memory and could tell you how much material they had, in order to play any concert, and he knew exactly where the material came from. He was the one who carried the only newspaper cutting that they received: it was from the local paper, the *Richmond and Twickenham Times*. And it was Brian who kept it carefully folded and tucked away. And he said, 'This is the only paper.' That paper he had even then tended to knock a bit. It tended to criticize them because they had the fans queuing outside this one hall on Saturday night, forcing the locals who were walking by, to walk out in the road. Although they gave a certain amount of credit to the band for being exciting and good and pulling people in, by the same token, they thought they were causing a good deal of trouble. But, he pointed up, that was the first time they'd ever been written about anyway. It was Brian, certainly, who laid down the guiding policy lines of the band. He told where their inspiration had come. He talked about Muddy Waters, Jimmy Reed, and people like that.

"He was in no way the sort of super-optismistic 'Let's shout around' type, in fact, he was proud of the band. He was very proud of the fact that he had built up this following in an outpost of London, where that kind of music wasn't really all that regular. The thing he *really* wanted to discuss with me was that nobody had taken any notice. Nobody had even thought they were good enough. Although Giorgio Gomelsky was not directly managing them, at least he was trying to get people down to see them. He was doing that good thing and for that reason I've always felt a bit guilty that I talked about the Rolling Stones to other people. What I should have done was written about them. Maybe got record companies interested, but *not* involved Andrew Oldham at that time. It was a bit unfair to Giorgio. Mick and Brian, though neither of them ever mentioned this at the time, felt that Giorgio was a kind of European madman, who was very artistic and shouted and ranted and so on. They didn't have much confidence in his ability. They also weren't too sure he believed that they *were* star material. But, from then on, it was Brian who reigned over every single move that happened to them in the months to come before there was any kind of break."

III

1962 was the year that Chubby Checker's "The Twist" started the dance craze, Bob Dylan received his first review in *The New York Times*, and Marilyn Monroe died.

The Rolling Stones performed at small clubs around London in 1962, including the Ricky Tick Club in Windsor. The Ricky Tick, located upstairs behind a pub, accommodated a very small crowd. Here Brian met Linda Lawrence, a tall and slender sixteen-year-old with a fine-boned face. A beatnik, Linda regularly hung out at the Ricky Tick. Jazz bands usually performed at the Club, but when the manager booked a group described as "rhythm 'n' blues-rock 'n' roll," Linda was curious. So were the other five people who showed up to hear the Rolling Stones. A few others straggled in during the show.

Brian played the harmonica. He attracted Linda's attention and seemed older than the other boys. Linda danced with some friends and chatted with him. During the band's break he talked to her enthusiastically about his music and invited her to London to visit him and to hear another performance.

Linda Lawrence and Brian liked each other immediately. "What I liked in him at first," Linda said, "was that he treated me like a lady. He was just so nice and polite; he looked after me. He was my first real relationship after leaving school. When I said, 'My parents would like to meet you,' he put on a clean shirt and washed up. And he was playing music. I like to be treated right and be respected, but on the other hand, I love music. I can just hang out and be crazy to a certain point. I liked the combination."

When Linda went for a visit to the Edith Grove apartment, Mick, Keith, and Brian were dissecting old blues records, trying to learn the techniques. As Donovan, who also learned to play the blues by listening to records, explained, "How to play the blues was a guarded secret. Nobody would teach you. Blues musicians wouldn't let you see the blues; they would turn their hands away while playing. So then these white boys who were trying to learn would have to listen to the records. And man, learning off the records was a lot of work."

Linda began attending hairdressing school in London. Brian suggested she become a fashion model. "Both Brian and I had difficulty fitting into society," Linda said. "Brian brought me to a London modeling school because he thought I would meet different kinds of people. So I took their course. Brian helped me (since he had thought of modeling), and took me to all the classes. Modeling was such a pushy thing. You had to do things you really didn't agree with (which is what you always have to do, I found out later). At the time, though, I didn't want to do anything unless I was totally happy doing it. Brian tried to interest me in some kind of work because he thought I had a direction too."

As Brian and Linda became more deeply involved, Pat Andrews was still hoping for any sort of relationship. She hung out at the coffee bars Brian and Linda frequented. Brian, concerned about Pat's capability to be a mother, told Linda he did not think Pat was capable of looking after their son, Julian Mark. He even asked Linda if she thought her parents might look after the child. Brian would tell Linda that he viewed his relationship with Pat as if "he needed a packet of cigarettes." Linda said: "Brian would look upon Pat as somebody to lean on and get looked after by. She worked and at one time gave him the cigarettes. It was that kind of a relationship."

Soon Mick, Keith, and Brian were running out of money and had to move from Edith Grove. Richard Hattrell, after a burst appendix, had moved back to Cheltenham. The other Stones found places to stay, but Brian, uncomfortable in the messy and chaotic Edith Grove apartment, had nowhere to live. When Linda's family invited him into their house, he welcomed the stability of a family home.

Brian lived with the Lawrences for over a year; first in Windsor, then in Reading. It is likely this was the first time in several years that Brian truly felt part of a family. The Lawrences breakfasted together. Brian wore Linda's brother's shirts. Her mother washed his clothes. Mr. and Mrs. Lawrence immediately took to Brian, especially Mr. Lawrence. He lent Brian the car and a bit of money when he needed it.

Brian felt the Lawrences accepted him. He bought them presents with his wages: a sun-shaped electric clock for the family, a purse with a bottle of perfume inside for Mrs. Lawrence. Linda, knowing that Brian was not a terribly generous person, was extremely pleased by his gifts to her family.

While living at the Lawrences, Brian wanted to introduce Linda to his parents, and hoped they would be impressed by her quiet and ladylike demeanor. Linda was the only girlfriend Brian ever brought home to meet his parents. "He thought I would please them," Linda said, "this quiet girl from the country. Our relationship was something to be proud of, like 'I'm going to get it together and everything's fine.' And we had a bigger Vauxhall than the Joneses. When we drove up to Brian's house, past Mr. Jones' Vauxhall, Mr. Jones immediately commented,

'Oh, you've got a Vauxhall.' And I said, 'Yeah, it's my dad's.' They were impressed with money. Especially in those little towns where if you pull in with a car that's a bit out of the ordinary, everyone looks at you."

Brian was so agitated and worried about visits home that upon reaching the outskirts of town, he would have an asthma attack. As Brian and Linda drove into Cheltenham, Brian made sounds as if he was going to vomit. He had to use his inhaler (which he carried with him at all times). Linda, too, carried an inhaler in case Brian lost his.

Severe asthma plagued Brian from early childhood until his death. Asthma attacks would beset him when he was unusually excited. In Windsor, Brian had attacks as often as three times a week. In later years, attacks would come almost daily. The asthma attack sets up a vicious cycle: it causes panic and a sensation of near-death by suffocation; that experience reinforces a feeling of anxiety, solitude, and fear.

Linda described him as "a very unhealthy person." Stew agreed: "There were quite a lot of things wrong with Brian . . . he was allergic to a lot of things. The thing with Brian was that he used to suffer very badly from asthma. He had great breathing problems and always carried an inhaler and pills. He seemed to be allergic to a lot of the standard sort of pills you get for this. . . . I remember back in 1963, long before people were taking drugs, Brian had to go to the hospital because somebody gave him some pills for something that was wrong with him, and his skin was literally falling off his arms."

Some people thought Brian appeared hostile when he performed but in reality he was terrified of having an asthma attack on stage. Judith Simonds, a London journalist, said, "Through his asthma, stage work was agony for him. Working to counteract his fear of an attack, he promoted the most unsmiling, violent image of the group."

The panic and asthma attack made little sense to Linda until she got to the Jones' house. "His parents are tight, straight, and empty," Linda said. "We walked in the house and it was as if Brian wasn't there. There was no voice or word between them. His father was a little warmer. He did react a little. Mr. Jones talked and got excited but then the mother kept trying to cool him. We took the Joneses to a pub. We thought that getting them out of the house would loosen them up; they would drink something and would want to talk. But they were still really tight."

"Brian's sister Barbara was a very straight, normal person. She was very nice. I only met her a couple of times. She wanted to be a schoolteacher. She was perfect for the parents—they loved her; she did everything right. Brian was probably jealous of her because she was doing everything they wanted. He never spoke much of her. She was perfect. She was religious and went to church every Sunday. Although Brian sang in the church choir, I don't think he was religious in that way."

Linda perceived that Lewis Jones was somewhat proud of Brian's musical achievements, but had trouble expressing it. Lewis felt pressured by the standards of his community and Brian's status as a rock star was not very respectable. What seemed to impress Lewis was that Brian was achieving *anything* at all.

Brian continually tried to win his father's approval and oriented his visits home toward that end. Linda recalls, "Brian really wanted to contact them. Some children will just leave and say, 'Well, they did me wrong. I don't want anything.' But I saw him keep attempting to bring something . . . he would play his music for them . . . . It wasn't hard for him to perform; he seemed proud of everything he took down there. His mother didn't really listen, but Lewis tried to. His father got excited and Brian would be happy about that, but then Lewis would pull back. After the music stopped, the atmosphere would return to its normal coldness. Then, they brought out pictures of Brian. As we all sat down, his mother said to me that Brian was a nice, normal kid. They showed me his report cards. His parents wanted him to climb up (to a higher middle-class) which is the most boring place in the world."

Brian's parents were only able to respond favorably to him as he became more successful. Linda said, "His parents ignored him. They never sent him any birthday cards or anything. Then as soon as he made a record, they sent him a pair of pajamas for his birthday. So the contact was because he had made it—money. But that wasn't the contact he was looking for. They would give him love if he gave them something physical. But I don't think they could give him the love which he thought it would bring out of them."

In 1963, Peter Jones, a freelance journalist working for *Record Mirror* contacted Andrew Loog Oldham, a nineteen-year-old publicist for Brian Epstein, after hearing the Stones at the Station Hotel. Andrew came to see the Stones with his partner, Eric Easton, and signed them on May 3, 1963. The deal was arranged between Brian and Oldham. Easton and Oldham managed the Stones until 1964 and then became their record producers.

Oldham's first managerial act was to get a release from the group's recording contract with I.B.C. Studio, where they had done the five unreleased tracks. Glyn Johns described the situation: "The two guys who owned the studio knew absolutely nothing about the record business. They didn't realize what they had on record. They took it to all the wrong people and failed to sell it in a week or two. Two weeks after the session, Eric Easton and Andrew Oldham appeared on the scene, saw the Stones, and said, 'Come with me, I'll make you a star!' And they did. The

Stones did have a contract, but Oldham and Easton paid ninety-three pounds to get them out of it, which shows what idiots the studio owners were."

One of the earliest changes Andrew Loog Oldham made was to remove Ian Stewart from the stage. He still played the piano for the Stones, but did not appear with them for club dates. Keith said, ". . . for us Stew [was] one part of the band up until Andrew. 'Well, he just doesn't look the part,' Andrew said, 'and six is too many for them [fans] to remember the faces in the picture.' "

At that time, Brian was acting as leader of the Stones. When he tried to comfort Stew about the change, Stew turned his anger into resentment for Brian. "Up until that time I used to play piano on stage," Stew said. "But they [Oldham and Easton] said, 'It looks all wrong.' So all right, all right . . . and Brian would always say, 'Don't worry about it. You're a part of the Stones. You'll always have a sixth of them.' And all this sort of rubbish. But I just ignored that."

Linda thought that Stew held Brian responsible for being taken off the stage. "Maybe Ian hated Brian because Ian stopped playing piano for awhile when they started getting famous," Linda said. "He may have blamed that on Brian because [he] was the leader. . . . Stewart was all right for a little while there, but he got bitter."

Relationships within the group fluctuated. As Brian's relationship with Stew degenerated, his friendship with Jagger blossomed. Brian and Mick shared their musical ideas freely, each influencing the other. According to Linda, Mick tried to help Brian when he could. One afternoon in 1963, Linda met Mick, Keith, and a few other friends on a street corner to go to the movies. She mentioned that she was thinking of leaving Brian; she had met someone else she liked better. As Linda was walking away,

Mick came around the corner screaming, "Oh, don't go! You'll just kill him!" The couple soon made up.

"I remember Mick always worrying a little about Brian's situation," Linda said. "He was the most sensitive toward Brian. Even when we [Linda and her husband, Donovan] saw Mick in 1974 I felt that he was the one saying, 'I could have done something, but I didn't. I wish I had.'"

However close Brian may have felt to Jagger, he could never overcome feeling threatened by him. The rivalry for leadership was an unspoken issue, but Brian felt the slow transfer of power to Mick. As Keith pointed out, "You don't realize it on stage, but the strength of the spotlight on the singer is so much brighter than that on the rest of the musicians. The focus of attention is paid so much on the singer that no matter how much you want to upstage the singer, you can't possibly do it."

The Rolling Stones, 1964.

Looking at those early photographs, it is clear that Brian was the only one capable of posing any threat to Jagger. Brian often looks straight-faced into the camera, quite beautiful and confronting; the others look slightly pubescent. His clothing is indicative of a personal style. He was beginning to set the style for a pop star. As Anita Pallenberg said in an interview many years later, "Brian was so far ahead of them you wouldn't believe it. Here are Mick and Keith up on the stage trying to be sex objects and Brian already [had] two illegitimate children. Brian was acting on it faster than anyone else; he knew his stuff very well."

According to Stew, another opportunity to get rid of Jagger presented itself in 1963 (they had previously thought about it after the Marquee gig), and Brian seized upon it: "Jagger has always had a weak voice, so he has to be careful if he wants to sing night after night. And this guy Easton, who didn't know anything about pop music, had seen Mick sing and said to Brian, 'I don't think Jagger is any good.' And so Brian said, 'Okay, we'll just get rid of him.' I feel sure Brian would have done it. It was Brian and myself in Easton's office and I said, 'Don't be so bloody daft!' "

Stew felt that Brian was incapable of leadership. He reasoned: "He didn't have it in him to be a leader. . . . And as soon as the group started to become in any way successful, Brian smelled money. He could sniff the fact that he was going to be a star. He wanted to be a star and do as little as possible. He was prepared to do anything that would make it; that would bring in money immediately. Whereas Mick and Keith weren't into that."

Another example of Brian's inability for leadership, according to Stew, was his lack of fairness: "When we started playin' gigs outside of London, Brian used to say, 'I'm the leader of this group and I think I'll stay at the best hotel. All the rest of you can stay in not such a good hotel. See?'

And, of course, they'd just laugh at him. And that was *it* from then on. It was all over for him as the leader. He started to isolate himself because of this attitude."

Although Keith agreed that Brian *said* he was going to stay at a better hotel, he never actually did. Keith related a different incident which he felt weakened Brian's leadership of the Stones: "The thing, and it's such a small thing, that we did find out in 1963, was that Brian had been drawing five pounds a week extra. He had this arrangement with Eric Easton, who was our manager, that Brian, as the leader of the band was therefore entitled to this five pounds extra each week. Everybody freaked out! And that actually was the beginning of the decline of Brian. In his defense, Brian did say that he did consider himself the leader and that he was justified. We said, 'Fuck you, talk about everybody being equal and what do we get for an example?' "

An undercurrent of cattiness definitely flowed within the Stones. Brian, because he was living in Windsor with Linda's family and had a more secure and proper lifestyle, alienated himself from the others. The boys teased him about living out in the country and driving a big Vauxhall. They probably didn't think he took it seriously, but Brian would come back from a gig feeling insecure and ask Linda if the other Stones liked him.

The Rolling Stones' first single "Come On" backed with "I Want to be Loved" was released in England on June 7, 1963. On September 19, 1963 the Rolling Stones began their first English tour, arranged by Andrew Oldham, which also featured Bo Diddley and the Everly Brothers. The Stones idolized Diddley and were excited about meeting him. Earlier in 1963, Brian and Keith spent hours going over Bo's music, trying to reproduce it. "Brian got into Bo Diddley," Keith said, "which I think was the best thing he ever got into on guitar. Brian's 'Mona (I Need You Baby)'

The early years. Mick Jagger, Brian, and Charlie Watts. Brian had named the group "Rollin' Stones" after a Muddy Waters' song, "Rollin' Stone Blues."

[on *The Rolling Stones*] was incredible. I never heard anybody before or since get that Bo Diddley thing down. Diddley himself was astounded. Bo said that Brian was the only cat he knew who'd worked out the secret of it."

When Bo arrived in London, Mick, Keith, and Brian gave him a set of gold cufflinks. Bo said, "It was my first engagement in England. Me, Brian, and Keith all became jug buddies: what we call jug buddies is that we drink out of the same jug. They were very nice to me then, like brothers. I don't mean black brothers, I mean brothers period. Togetherness. And it was really unique. These people showed me the hospitality of another country."

"When I met Brian, he was playing slide guitar and harmonica. His slide guitar was great. Especially to be as young as he was. Brian was a little dude that was trying to pull the group ahead. I saw him as the leader. He didn't take no mess. He was a fantastic cat. He handled the group beautifully."

"Linda Lawrence came on the tour and did my sister's hair. Brian was the only one that had his girlfriend there. They were planning on getting married."

Linda said, "I went everywhere. The other Stones would get uptight because they wouldn't want to take their girlfriends everywhere. They argued about it. I remember one of Mick's girlfriends, Chrissie Shrimpton, would always tell me, 'Oh, Linda you can't go because we can't go.' She would get real pissed off because I would get in with Bo and the Duchess [Bo's sister].

"Bo knew that we were in love. He was upset when we split up. Bo was so beautiful to Brian. He was getting off on teaching Brian things. Bo would say, 'You move like this when you're on stage.' And he showed Mick how to move his legs. This was during their rehearsals. That's when I thought everything was great; when Brian met the people like Bo Diddley whose records he had listened to over and over."

In the beginning of 1964, the Stones, who had been signed to Decca, were about to release "Not Fade Away," which would become their first hit single. That year, they would also release their first album, *The Rolling Stones.* It sold phenomenally well. They were extremely busy with live performances: ninety-nine concerts to promote the record—which meant being on the road almost constantly.

The Rolling Stones had become the hottest band in London. Coming from provincial Cheltenham, Brian had dreamed of making it in London. "His original aspiration," Keith Richard said, "was to make it in the London club circuit. That was his ultimate ambition. Whereas for Mick and me, coming from London [the suburbs], that was the first thing to do. After that we really had to take it further uphill. Brian peaked when we were the hottest band in London."

Brian loved the music they were making and all the performing. His guitar playing was authoritative. Keith went on to become expert in his own way, but in late 1963 he played enthusiastically rather than brilliantly. Brian had also attracted a large following, mostly women. Linda described Brian's musicianship: "His guitar work on stage and off was so amazing. It was a feeling coming out of it that *he* was putting into it. I felt it was something that came out of him from all the pain that he'd been through. The Blues. It was like a whine or a cry."

As the Stones became more popular in London, Brian was the one on stage who was unforgettable. As Giorgio Gomelsky has said of Brian, "He had a very good sense of tactics. He knew how to get an audience. He knew what noises to make to be heard." Alexis elaborated on Brian's stage presence: "Insofar as announcements were concerned and everything early on, it was Mick who riled people up. But when it came to an actual performance, the aggressive member of the Stones was Brian. He would, very deliberately, work up an audience. He wouldn't be rude to them with words like Mick. He would needle. Here is a typical example: the Stones would leave an audience waiting, even when they were fairly new and working the club circuit. They'd be an hour late. And the audience would get all fed up and nasty. Then the Stones would come on stage. Mick would drop his lip, and dribble a little bit. And look as if, 'Well, that's done you some fuckin' good anyway, we might play a little later sort of thing.' And get the audience really worked up. But once they started performing, Mick would just sing. He wouldn't actually be aggressive. But Brian would do that funny tip-toe dance of his right to the edge of the stage, and he'd slap his tambourine in the audience's face as if to say, 'Fuck you!' Then he'd drop back again, leering at you all the time, so as to make you really angry.

The meteoric success of the Beatles was a great influence on Brian; their popularity intensified his desire to be a star. Brian wanted to be a star because Brian *needed* to be a star. Linda said, "He felt he *had* to be a star because he wasn't a star in his family; he wanted to be a star in another way. It wasn't his ego. It was something he wanted to fulfill . . . hadn't got from his childhood."

Mick told a reporter for *Creem* magazine: "That was the thing that fucked Brian up—because he was so desperate for attention. He wanted to be admired and loved and all that . . . which he was by a lot of people, but it was never enough for him." Whatever approval Brian received was never to fill the inner emptiness that fed on failure.

Giorgio Gomelsky was responsible for the introduction of the Beatles to the Rolling Stones. During the Beatles first visit to London, Giorgio suggested they catch the Stones' performance at the Crawdaddy Club. According to reports, knowing that the Beatles were coming made the Stones very nervous. After the gig the two groups went back to Mick and Keith's place and talked all night.

When the Beatles played their first concert at the Royal Albert Hall, Giorgio brought the Rolling Stones there. After the show, when everyone had left, Brian Jones, Giorgio, and several others (no roadies yet) helped carry the guitars and amplifiers to the stage door. There was a mob of excited but orderly teenagers waiting, replete with scraps of paper and pens. The fans, seeing Brian's long hair, thought he was a Beatle, and rushed up to him to get his autograph. Brian relished signing his name and as they were leaving he whispered to Giorgio, "This is what I want."

Keith also remembers the first time they saw the Beatles at Albert Hall: "Brian, very impressed with the Beatles' success, fancied himself a backup vocalist. He was really hot into this thing of harmonies, which is something we never touched before. I mean, Mick did all the singing, we did all the playing, and that was it. It was always forbidden to sing. Brian would work out these incredible harmonies with Bill [Wyman]. He got us doing all these songs that he really didn't know anything about. Mick and I knew that the band wasn't really capable; wasn't the right instrumentation to play that kind of stuff. The Beatles got away with it because . . .they carried it through. They didn't play it any better than us—probably not as well most of the time—but their vocals were together. There's no way we needed to compete on that level because there were other things that Brian could do. Brian's voice was not his forte. It wasn't bad. It was never out of tune. It just didn't have any dynamics to it. It was like a rasp. . . .

"After seeing the Beatles and this incredible show, which was at the height of English Beatlemania before America, he was completely overawed by them. The whole purist thing went right out the window and suddenly he wanted to be a rock 'n' roll star."

Keith's statement, "It was always forbidden to sing," is a telling one. It shows that the group's democratic process had serious flaws—and these were previously blamed on Brian. Who forbade the rest of the Stones to sing? Was it Andrew? Was it Mick?

Stew related another incident concerning Brian's desire to sing: "One of the first gigs we ever did outside of London was a place in the north of England called Sunderland. The other group on the bill was probably the Hollies, or one of those groups from up there that had this close harmony. Three part singin'. So Brian said to me, 'I've got to have three singers. I want a microphone.' And he couldn't sing to save his life."

In the late fall of 1963, Linda found out that she was pregnant. At her parents' urging, Brian and Linda decided to visit the Joneses and tell them about their expected grandchild. "Brian was scared stiff to tell them anything," Linda said. "We went through the whole visit and never told them, because we felt that cold feeling. There was no opening. Yet we came down all ready to tell them. Finally, when Brian wrote them about it, they denied it and cut me right off. They said, 'Oh, it's not his.' They thought I was terrible because I was pregnant, but they had accepted me before. I had slept in their house. Getting pregnant was just the whole wrong approach to them because of their way of life. It wasn't the way they expected it. I felt very bad and Brian freaked out."

Brian and Linda considered the possibility of an abortion. "We saw a doctor," Linda said. "Shirley (Charlie Watts' girlfriend) took Brian and me to see someone. The doctor took us aside individually and asked, 'Are you in love?' And we both said, 'Yes!' And the doctor said, 'Go home then. We're not going to do it.'"

During the months of Linda's pregnancy, the couple

With Linda Lawrence, Windsor, 1963.

lived in Windsor in relative calm and happiness, even though Brian had brief rages of jealousy over her male friends. "Brian never thought he was good-looking," Linda said. "He thought all those big, dark-haired beatnik guys I used to hang out with were much better looking. On one occasion Brian gave me a black eye and I had to tell my dad I walked into a door. I had gone to a party with an old boyfriend to see some old friends. Brian had heard I had done other things too, so he hit me. When he got upset, violence came out, but afterwards he would feel guilty and act extra nice. I never felt that he was cruel, but that he was releasing something instead; that something from his past had made him angry. I knew Brian could only release those feelings in front of me."

Brian vented many of his frustrations on Linda. Some of his mischievous play bordered on the sadistic: "When we were living in Windsor, we would go for boat rides down the river," Linda said. "Brian took me to the edges of waterfalls and would really scare the life out of me—get right close to the edge and then swerve back. Every time I felt terrified. Or else he'd drive the car to the middle of nowhere, get out, lock the doors, and pretend he was someone scary."

Brian liked to flirt with danger but could not commit himself to a long-term relationship with it. Only when he became conscious of his self-destructiveness would he change the course of his behavior. One incident may help to explain the situation. Brian had always liked the feeling of power in a fast car. He took Linda out in a Jaguar for a trial run. As they sped off, rain began to fall. Suddenly a cat darted in their path. Brian slammed on the brakes and the car skidded and turned over. Bruised and shaken, neither Brian nor Linda were seriously injured. Terrified, Brian decided not to buy *that* car or *any* car. After the incident, Mr. Lawrence drove him to the band's gigs.

England's Newest Hitmakers. 1964.

IV

In 1964, the British Invasion hit America. The Beatles arrived in February to tour and perform on *The Ed Sullivan Show*. Their single "I Want to Hold Your Hand" and their album *Meet the Beatles* reached the #1 spot. By April, the Beatles had five singles and two albums at the top of the charts. Meanwhile, the Stones were finishing a tour around Great Britain. Although Brian was excited by the touring, he missed Linda greatly. He wrote her the following letter when he was in Manchester and she was with her family in Windsor:

Manchester, Wed.

My darling Linda,

I'm so very, very sorry I haven't written until now—but really we've been so busy and you know I hate writing letters anyway. The tour is proving a great laugh but playing in theaters is definitely a drag. We've had a lot of fun and met many people. I'm sorry I didn't ring you on Saturday night. I tried again and again but the connections with London were broken and I couldn't get through—Honestly darling, that's the truth.

The new record will be out soon—it's great—we wrote the "B" side! It's called "Stoned"!! I'll play you the copy of it when we come back—can I stay with you next *Monday*? We're coming back on *Sunday* night—Can we stay in Windsor perhaps?—Reading. We shall have to be off again on Tuesday morning.

Honestly Darling I can't wait to see you again. Although you may have given up hope. I love you so very much. I always think about you and wonder what you are doing and who you are with—I don't trust you an inch! I'm being good and haven't broken my promise—and I won't do either!

We played in Hull last night at a concert with Johnny Kidd and the Pirates and Heintz. The girls were mad—the screaming nearly split my eardrums—we stole the show. We have to be up early tomorrow (I'm writing this in bed on Wednesday night) to go to Scotland.

Do you remember the Mindbenders —Wayne Fontana's mob? Well, do you remember the coats they had at Watford that night they came to see us? The grey check ones with black collars, pockets, etc.—I bought one today—it's real gear. I like it better than my leather one and that's good! Did you buy one for your birthday?

I wish I could be with you on your birthday darling—but I'll be thinking about you all the time. Now, will you be in Windsor on *Friday* night and I'll ring about two o'clock in the morning—I *presume* from Newcastle.

Well, my darling, I'll tell you all the rest when I ring you up on Friday. *Please* be good and faithful and don't forget all about me. I love you more than ever darling and I *always* will.

Bye sweetheart,
Brian

The song Brian refers to in the letter (called "Stoned") was the B-side of their second single. The A-side was written by John Lennon and Paul McCartney, and it was called "I Wanna Be Your Man."(The story goes that Lennon and McCartney wrote the song in fifteen minutes.) Brian's slide guitar work on that song was outstanding.

When the Stones returned to London, they recorded songs for a BBC radio program called *Saturday Club* which was broadcast on Saturday mornings. The boys performed four songs, only one take on each. The burgeoning rock 'n' roll industry was just learning how to deal with its stars. Individual artists had little control over their music. The Beatles and the Stones were the first groups that wanted to make decisions about their music, an unheard-of option at that time. "At that point, 'artistes' were treated far differently than they are now," Keith said. "Up until the Beatles and us, it was absolutely ludicrous that the performer should choose the material he was gonna sing. The producer would absolutely pick it for you. In America, even in the mid-seventies, it [was] still practiced very much, for example, with the Philly sound. The Stylistics and those groups are told note for note what's to be sung [by the producer]. The guys are absolutely straight off the street corner. They have beautiful voices, but the producer puts everything together. He tells them how to sing every inflection, so they never thought that the artist *could* choose what he was gonna sing [and] on top of that, how it was going to be played, what instrumentation was gonna be used. That was somebody else's decision, the record company's place in the whole thing."

"The embryonic music scene was perfect for a bright, ambitious hustler to forge out a path for the Rolling Stones. Obviously the Stones were not going to be told "note for note what's to be sung." But their personal charisma and music *were* malleable and marketable for Andrew Loog Oldham, who had a vision of a new direction for rock 'n' roll. He became a winner at what Keith Richard called "the only cockfight left: Rock 'n' Roll."

The Rolling Stones began working on their first album for Decca. It was recorded on a machine the size of a Sony cassette tape recorder. On this album, *The Rolling Stones*, Brian played the most diverse part. He sang, played guitar, and harmonica. He is the most distinct figure in the album cover photograph, wearing a white shirt and vest, while the others have on sports jackets. Brian and Mick are more prominent as they flank the other three Stones. It was ironic that in England, this album had neither the title, nor the name of the band on it. You had to ask for "the new Rolling Stones album." This was unheard-of in the record industry, and the American label placed the headline "England's Newest Hitmakers" across the top of the front cover. Included on the back of the album cover was one of Andrew Oldham's famous statements, "The ROLLING STONES are more than just a group—they are a way of life."

The record showcases Brian's early slide guitar work, most remarkably on "I'm a King Bee." Brian also attacks the harmonica on "Not Fade Away," making it moan and shout and sometimes sound like train whistles. During the break on "Not Fade Away," Keith plays lead guitar off Brian's lead harmonica and they trade back and forth. Brian broke rock tradition by using the harmonica as a lead instrument.

On lead harmonica, Hollywood Palace *TV show, 1964. Brian was the first rock performer to use the harmonica as a lead instrument.*

Andrew Oldham was not known at that time for his expertise in record production (although that was no reflection on his abilities as a publicist or manager), so when he appeared at I.B.C. Recording Studio to buy the Stones out of their contract (for the five unreleased tracks), he tried to convince Glyn Johns to engineer the records. (An engineer technically achieves a sound on record. Some engineers, however, like Glyn, become so deeply involved with the music that their personality imprints distinctly on the record.) "I would not continue working with the Rolling Stones," Glyn said, "because Andrew had turned up and taken them. In my opinion, Andrew Oldham couldn't produce juice from a bloody orange. So I said to Andrew, 'The day you can prove to me that you can produce a record, then I will come and engineer. 'Till then good afternoon.' "

A popular story related that after the first recording session with the Stones, Andrew told the engineer to give him the tapes. The engineer said incredulously, "Don't you want to mix them?"

"What do you mean, mix them?" Andrew asked.

"Well . . . they're all on different tracks."

The Stones, of course, were as green as Andrew and because they had little recording experience, they didn't know the limitations of his recording skill. "What we didn't realize," Keith said, "was that Andrew knew absolutely nothing about recording. We thought he was a producer, when in actual fact, he was learning as he went along just like us. Whereas Phil Spector learned his trade from the bottom up, slowly pulling these incredible strokes at Liberty Records and getting his thing together with the Crystals and the Ronettes, Andrew *imagined* himself to be like this. It's like someone off the street saying they wanted to produce records. Andrew would go into the studio and have absolutely no idea what to do. He would bluff it. That's what he did with us, and that's what we did with him. Except we were playing gigs every night. A band that works on the road every night is a hot band."

Stew also agrees that Andrew's forte was not as a record producer: "He only slipped up when he wanted to be a record producer. The albums credit him with being the

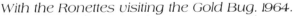

With the Ronettes visiting the Gold Bug. 1964.

producer when . . . Andrew's musical ideas were just adding tambourines and girl singers. We went to the Chess
One Recording Studio in Chicago and RCA in Hollywood
[to record the second album *12 x 5*] where they have good
engineers and know what they're doing. They resent
somebody saying do this, that, and the other thing."

During early 1964, the Stones verged on international
success. Shortly after the release of their album in May in
America (it was released in April in England) they toured
America for the first time. Brian told *New Musical Express*
in an interview on May 29, 1964, "Now we're going to
America and I think I've finally proved to those people
who said I was doing the wrong thing that I've been right
all along."

With their growing success, Brian doubted if he could
be himself *and* be a star. Did he need to out-do Mick? Was
being Brian Jones enough? These questions nagged at Brian
and began to build when the band started receiving fan
mail. Brian would ask Linda, "Who do you think gets the
most fan letters after the show? Do you think Mick is
better than me? Do the fans like that type of person better?" Brian would stand in front of the mirror at Linda's
house saying, "Mick does this, so I think I'll do the
same. . . . And what do you think I ought to wear for the
chicks?" At times Brian would cry because he felt that he
was losing control of the band that he had started. "I remember when Brian and I would talk about his feelings of
insecurity," Linda said, "that the boys were one way and
he was another. He would question whether the fans came
to see the Stones because of Mick, the way he was presenting the show (theatrics), or did they come because of the
actual music, which was what I felt Brian was represent-
ing."

"As long as Brian and I were together he thought of

himself as the leader of the group. After I left, the records started coming out and everything was reversed. It was a complete Mick-and-Keith thing. Brian must have foreseen that he would be pushed out because he talked about it. Brian looked for ways to stop it or make it right. He always tried to find something to hang on to."

"Not Fade Away" backed with "Little by Little" became the Stones' first hit single. It was slated to be a hit the moment it was released, courtesy of Oldham's skillful manipulation of the press. If the Beatles were the "boys you love," then the Stones were the "boys you love to hate." In terms of celebrity, Andrew did nothing but good for the Stones. Recently, writer David Dalton wrote: "Because the Beatles were an already established group and the Stones were virtually unknown, comparisons between the two could only work to the Stones' advantage. The press was programmed in a subtle, or often not so subtle manner by Andrew's Law: for every star there is an anti-star. For every Elvis there is a Pat Boone . . . for every Beatles there must be a Rolling Stones." In addition, Phil Spector was involved in the production of "Not Fade Away" and his presence drew press attention to the band.

Four months after the Beatles hit America the Rolling Stones left England to do the same. The U.S. was still in the throes of Beatlemania. In 1964, the Stones opened in San Bernadino as headliners. They were accompanied by Bobby Vee, The Chiffons, Bobby Goldsboro, and Bobby

The Rolling Stones in New York. 1964.

Comstock. The Stones played San Antonio, Minneapolis, Omaha, Detroit, Pittsburgh, Harrisburg, Pa., and finished at Carnegie Hall in New York. When the Stones landed at Kennedy Airport in New York at the start of the tour, screaming crowds of fans broke through a police cordon, trying to reach the band. Several days later, the Rolling Stones were officially introduced on American television by Dean Martin. Martin made fun of the way they looked and was grabbing at any laugh he could get—at their expense: "Their hair is not long," he announced. "It's just smaller foreheads and higher eyebrows." He led into a commercial by saying, "Now don't go away anybody. You wouldn't want to leave me with these Rolling Stones, would you?" But the most insulting remark was Martin's reference to a trampoline artist performing on the show: "That's the father of the Rolling Stones. He's been trying to kill himself ever since."

The boys were very naive about touring and their main excitement during the trip was to buy some good American blues records. As had happened to the Beatles, America offered them wild liquor-filled parties strewn with available women. As Keith said to Robert Greenfield of *Rolling Stone* magazine, "Nobody realizes how America blew our minds and the Beatles' too. Can't even describe what America meant to us."

Brian loved performing on that first U.S. tour. He danced on stage, his harmonica moaning, flipping his head back and tossing his long blond hair. He usually wore a suit at the concerts and after he took his jacket off, he looked rather dandyish in his vest. A woman who attended the concert described him: "Brian had so much energy. You could see him really getting high behind the music, especially when he played harmonica. It *completely* turned him on. It was almost like Mick Jagger's spotlight was Brian Jones' equally. There was the harmonica and there were some guitar runs; then Mick would do a little dance and take the maracas right to the edge of the stage. And the music flowed (between) all five of them. Even Charlie got off his drum set and introduced a few numbers."

On his return Brian told Linda, "America was parties and everything that you could possibly dream of. It was all there, laid on us."

Brian sent Linda tourist postcards from different towns. The first one was from "Moon-Lit" Minneapolis:

> *Darlin' Lindy,*
> READ THIS ONE FIRST—
> Here we go with the postcards.
> I've been buying but haven't
> sent any—so you can have
> them all at once! All my love,
>
> *Brian*

Another from Minneapolis with a picture of the First National Building:

Greetings from
MINNEAPOLIS
MINN.

> How's Pip [the poodle he had bought for Linda]? Hope he's O.K. America's really a gas! I'll soon be home to see you.
>
> *Love,*
> *Brian*

The next card pictured
the Chicago River:

You can't complain that I haven't sent
any postcards can you? Give my love to
your Mum and Dad.

Brian

Two from Omaha:

I really miss Texas. The weather
was so hot and everything was great.
I killed a rattlesnake too! I've got
this rattler for you! I'm looking
forward to seeing you.

Bye,
Brian

This is where I am now. Life is so happy
here. I don't want to come back to
England ever—except to get you
and Pip and Billy [the goat he
had bought for Linda].

Love,
Brian

He also sent his parents the following postcard:

Dear Mum and Dad,
 America's just about the greatest place
I've ever seen. We've just been to Atlanta
and N.Y. and Chicago. I'm having a
fantastic time. If you want to come over
I've just got to send you some tickets and
you can come over. Really great, sorry I
didn't write sooner.

       Love,
       Brian

As soon as the Stones started attracting enormous crowds, Brian's ambivalence about performing became more pronounced. He was fearful of the wild energy that the Stones drew from their audiences. As the crowd hysteria grew, so did Brian's dread of being at the mercy of the wildly screaming, weeping teenagers. But he also enjoyed a tremendous sense of power from the manipulation of thousands of people. He sensed the danger that the audience could turn on them. And although that never happened, Brian did question how far the band's control extended.

Even in 1963, when the audience had only numbered in the hundreds, Brian feared them. A few times, Brian phoned Mr. Lawrence after a gig saying, "Please come and get me. I'm scared to go out because of all the people." At a concert in Dublin about thirty people leaped over the orchestra pit onto the stage and turned a performance into a riot. Brian wrestled with three punching teenagers while Mick was dragged to the floor. Police and stagehands tried to control the situation by flinging fans off-stage into the pit. The next night in Belfast they had ambulances standing by. When the Stones went into "Satisfaction" the audience went wild. Fans were jumping up and down on the seats until seventy to eighty seats collapsed. Pieces of seats, ashtrays, and bits of iron were hurled onto the stage. The toll was at least two serious leg injuries, innumerable cases of fainting, and one youth whose face was covered with blood from a head injury.

Both the Beatles and the Stones learned early in their careers not to wear scarfs or chains around their necks for fear of being choked. "Whether Beatlemania was any more crazy than Stonemania was a debatable point," Keith said. "It was just pure insanity. It was all those things you saw on those Monkee TV programs six years later—but it was really true. Zooming down laundry chutes into baskets in hotels. Incredible! Just to be stopped from being ripped to pieces by these chicks. And Brian was terrified. He had this fear of the scene, which to us was overdone. But everybody dealt with it in his own way. Usually the car would arrive at the theater and Brian would see thousands of chicks milling around. He'd say, 'Driver, driver, look at them. Slow down a little.' Then he'd get into this incredible panic state. Everybody said, 'Take it easy, Brian.' He was petrified. The first time we went to America in '64, Murray the K [he late N.Y. disc-jockey] and 'Fifth Beatle' instigated this really nasty thing. I mean, he did it to boost himself and us: he had these chicks running around New York with scissors trying to get a lock of our hair. Brian was *terrified!*"

Their first American tour ended in July of 1964. A few weeks later Linda gave birth to Julian Brian. During the earlier months of her pregnancy Brian was considerate and solicitous of Linda's health. Still, with touring and band pressures, the pregnancy weighed heavily on the couple. They discussed getting married and even priced a few houses, but Brian felt much too overwhelmed by his fast-moving career to concentrate on domestic problems. He hurried from one event to another with little connection between them.

In the second half of 1964, the Stones were "happening." They released three singles which instantly became hits: "Tell Me" in June, "It's All Over Now" in July, and "Time Is on My Side" in September. On these singles, Brian played rhythm guitar. Their second album, *12 x 5*, was released in October. Brian played slide guitar on "Grown Up Wrong," and absolutely magnificent harmonica on "2120 South Michigan Avenue." In November, the Stones released the single "Little Red Rooster" (in England only). It was Brian's favorite Stones' track featuring his impeccable slide guitar, and it turned out to be the Stones' last blues single. The single "Heart of Stone" was released in December. Around this time the Stones also recorded "I Can't be Satisfied," which was not released in America until 1972, even though it was out in England on their second album in 1964. Critic Robert Palmer, wrote of this cut in *Rolling Stone:* "Jones was playing excellent bottleneck guitar as far back as 1964. His use of the slide's harmonic potential behind Jagger's unusually authoritative voice is worth hearing again and again. He underlines words with whooping washes of metallic sound while Richard plays a characteristically lean backup figure."

In addition to the time in the studio, the Rolling Stones were busy promoting their records with tours. They toured England from August through October, and America again in October and November.

Three months after Julian's birth the second American tour began. Brian was again dazzled by a whole new way of life. Being a father and husband, and a rock rock 'n' roll star seemed impossible. Constantly running from interview to concert to TV show robbed Brian of precious time for reflection about his private life and relationship with Linda. Frequently overloaded, tired and confused, Brian shifted between emotional extremes. He would be loving and joking one minute, viciously screaming angry words the next with, what seemed to Linda, little provacation.

On one occasion, Brian struck Linda for no reason. She remembered, "He hit me in an elevator once, just because he was so mad. I hadn't done anything (although I always used to think it was because of something I had done). He would change so quickly."

"A lot of the time, Brian really didn't know who he was," Alexis said. "[He] was very finely balanced from the nervous point of view, very finely balanced indeed. He was given to 100 percent shifts of reaction in a matter of seconds. It was very obvious he had problems controlling his own head at times. He was intelligent enough to be able to work out certain things to save himself, but without the desire to do them. He was also into that thing which a lot of us are into: when you get into a particularly dangerous path you want to know how far you can survive it. In relationships with others as well as in relationship with himself he had this funny on-and-off balance."

Brian's performing tactics reflected this "on-and-off balance." He would saunter to the lip of the stage, playing his guitar or tambourine and tease the audience to riot— enticing them to jump onto the stage. Then he would casually drop back to his position next to Mick, seemingly oblivious to what he had just done.

The interaction of the group itself was an undeniable source of Brian's troubles. Despite his early involvement with Andrew Oldham, Brian was frustrated and saddened by Oldham's influence. Andrew, as the group's manager, wielded enormous power over the band, and Brian was a purist: According to Hattrell, "Brian would rather play to two people who appreciated what he was doing than to two thousand that were screaming their heads off. He was a real musician." Andrew's main concern and job as man-

L–R: *Keith Richard, Mick Jagger, Bill Wyman, Charlie Watts, and Brian. Glasgow, September, 1966.*

ager, however, was marketing the Stones. He thought of Brian's purism as silly; that Brian was hung-up on one particular kind of music with the narrow-minded intensity of a stamp collector. Brian thought of Andrew as a fly-by-night flash, a musical trash can. "Brian never liked Andrew," Keith said. "But he knew that Andrew could help the band more than anybody else. Andrew pulled all the right strokes as far as public relations were concerned, at just the right time. And it worked like clockwork. Nothing was planned. It just fell into place and Brian was resigned to the fact that Andrew was a necessary part of the general non-communicativeness."

Typical of Andrew's publicity maneuvers was to deliberately make a public display of a relatively innocuous incident. After a concert, the Stones stopped at a gas station to use the bathroom. The attendant told the Stones that they couldn't use the private restroom because the toilets were being repaired. Then, according to a story in the *Express*, they urinated against the boundary wall of the service station "without taking steps to conceal this act." When the mechanic asked them to leave, Mick, Brian, and Bill started chanting and gyrating around the gas station. Nobody knows who called the cops, but the three were found guilty of disorderly behavior and fined a total of thirty pounds. This incident could have easily gone unnoticed unless someone wanted to capitalize that sort of publicity.

According to the newspaper article, Brian seemed a willing participant in this incident. However, Peter Jones, a prominent British music journalist, was certain he was not. "When Andrew was formulating his plan for the Rolling Stones, [with slogans like 'Would you let your sister go out with a Rolling Stone?' or 'The Stones are a group parents love to hate.']" Jones said, "Brian put forward the constructive ideas. Brian thought that some of the anti-establishment, anti-authoritarian lines that Andrew fed the press went too far."

"There were a lot of things that Andrew regarded as triumphs of promotion, in terms of getting space for the Rolling Stones, that did upset Brian. He was afraid of constantly being photographed in angry and aggressive poses. The sensitive side of Brian Jones made him think that the Rolling Stones were in danger of being classified as morons when he knew a clear amount of intelligence ran through the band. And although these things were good in terms of gimmickry, Brian resented a lot of it."

Brian was the first Stone to challenge Andrew's basic image-building authority. He would phone Andrew (often after fortifying himself with alcohol) to say, "Look, let's just change this photographer. He has a one-dimensional approach." Brian was trying to say, "Yes, we are anti-establishment, but we aren't anti-everything." And to Brian, the Rolling Stones gradually became caricatures of themselves.

"The Rolling Stones were building a reputation as the sort of group that never could be relied upon," Peter Jones said. "In other words, you'd never ask a Rolling Stone to do a favor for a charity or sign autographs."

One particular afternoon in 1964, Andrew publicly stated that the Rolling Stones did not sign autographs and did not have orderly queues of fans. Brian never accepted this: at roughly the same time as Andrew's public proclamation, the Stones played an all-star Sunday Show at Wembley Stadium Pool, to ten thousand people. The security brigade would not let the fans through to the big backstage area. Nor would they allow the artists through to meet the fans. Peter Jones came in through that backstage area with great difficulty. Since many of the fans knew he was connected with the Rolling Stones, they gave him pieces of paper to get autographed. When Peter told Brian about the number of people backstage and how long they had been waiting, Brian talked the security guards into allowing the fans to form a gap between the stage door and himself so he *could* sign autographs. And although the Stones were rushing off to the north of England for a gig that same evening, Brian nervously signed autographs for over an hour.

Peter Jones was one of the writers for the Stones' British fan magazine, the *Rolling Stone Monthly* (not to be confused with *Rolling Stone* magazine founded by Jann Wenner). The magazine defended the Stones against the tabloids, the national press, and the television that depicted the Stones as aggressive, rough young men who didn't give a damn about authority. "Whenever there was an all-in meeting for the *Rolling Stone Monthly*," Jones said, "we'd get the writers and the Stones all together around a dressing room table. If the conversation got into the outrageous 'Let's feed this story to them—the line that Andrew would take—Brian would just keep out of it. It was as if he lost interest as soon as things got beyond the realm of commonsense."

> *IT WAS REALLY AN UNHOLY TRINITY BETWEEN MICK, KEITH, AND ANDREW OLDHAM.*
>
> —Ian Stewart

Brian looked, unsuccessfully, for support within the group. "He knew that Bill and Charlie weren't gonna say very much," Peter Jones said. "They're more like employees; always on the outside looking in and not wanting to get involved. Meanwhile, Mick and Keith were becoming a real team with Andrew Oldham." Stew also saw the factionalism within the group: "Andrew is very shrewd and Mick's very shrewd. They got on extremely well all the way down the line as to how things should be done. In those days Keith never used to say very much but he would always go along with Mick."

And, as Jones continued, "I think it must have taken a fair amount of nerve as the months went by to speak out against Andrew, because Andrew didn't listen to anybody who said that he was going along on the wrong course."

Brian turned to older more established music people for help. "Brian was the one," Jones said, "who did take outside advice into account. He wasn't like Mick and Keith who thought 'This is what we're going to do and this is obviously right because we say so.'"

It seems that Brian was thinking along the lines of: "Look, we're all new to this. There are a lot of people around who have seen all this happen before;. who have seen groups like us come up and go down. They *do* know something. Later on we may take no notice of their advice, but for the moment we should listen." When Andrew wanted to put out a story suggesting that the Stones had done something outrageous, Brian asked Peter Jones and other journalists if they would be taken in by this publicity, or if they would think this story was mere hustling for space? Brian asked whether the emerging public conception of the Rolling Stones would enable them to stay on top; he feared that the image would submerge the music. "He was terrified of being dated," Jones said, "that after the *image* was done, the *music* would be done, and people wouldn't take the Stones seriously. Brian especially felt this way after Andrew Oldham made one of his famous speeches that the 'Rolling Stones are not just a band but a way of life.' And that way of life cut across their individual backgrounds and across the voice of authority. Brian questioned this all the way."

Class consciousness always operated within the Stones, and the band's caustic image helped sharpen those differences between Mick, Keith, and Brian. Alexis Korner is certain that Mick has always attributed great meaning to social class: "Mick used to be suspicious of me because I wasn't working-class and he once said to me, 'Man, the Blues is working-class music.' To which I said, 'Aw, come on, you and your bloody London School of Economics. What are you talking about?' People were suspicious of my band because I had two Cambridge graduates in the horn section."

"The class thing in music is very heavy. Before the Second World War, your great way out, in terms of class or race, was to become world heavyweight titleholder. No one cares about the class of the world heavyweight titleholder; no one cares about the class of the superstar."

The burgeoning image of the Stones portrayed them as men who scorned manners and propriety, laughed at education and cursed at respect. Of course, this description rallied behind bravado and cynicism. These attitudes made Brian painfully conscious of his genteel middle-class background. Brian was the Rolling Stone who had the most trouble reconciling their professed values—yet in some ways he lived them to the fullest. He fathered at least three illegitimate children, was busted twice, suffered from nervous breakdowns and dressed the most outrageously. Brian lived out the lyrics of the Rolling Stones' songs like "19th Nervous Breakdown," "Mother's Little Helper," "Ride on Baby," and "No Expectations." If they were not written specifically about Brian, they paralleled his life.

Andrew's idea of having Mick and Keith write songs for the Stones contributed most to Brian's demise as the primary Stone. One of the tragedies of Brian's life as a Stone was that he just could not put a song together. "Andrew's pushing Mick and Keith to write songs was what really caused Brian to be left behind," Glyn Johns said. "Until that time Brian was pretty much the group's spokesman and had some very good musical ideas. He was really incredible. A lot of Rolling Stones records were built on riffs and Brian invariably played those riffs (on songs such as 'Diddley Daddy,' 'Roadrunner,' 'Bright Lights, Big City,' 'I Want to be Loved,' and 'Honey What's Wrong?' Then Mick and Keith were encouraged to write and sell their songs and the whole onus of the Rolling Stones shifted to [them]. They and Andrew took over directing the band. The songwriting naturally drew Mick and Keith closer together. Charlie and Bill didn't matter because they didn't want to get involved and had no spin-off things like songwriting."

Keith, too, agrees that this was the turning point, musically, in his relationship with Brian. "Things got more complicated," Keith said, "when Andrew got Mick and me together to write songs. It was the final full circle back to Mick and I being more together, and Brian feeling the tension. Andrew literally forced Mick and I to start writing songs. We hadn't even thought about it, it was just one of his intuitive guesses that worked for some reason. Andrew presented the idea to us, not on any sort of artistic level, but more money. He sort of said, 'You aren't going to get it together just recording other people's songs. Every Liverpool band is doing that. You gotta start writing songs and you gotta start sending them to other people.' Mick and I, apart from the Stones thing (which we were really into) were also writing songs for Andrew to sell for Gene Pitney and those other people that Andrew had his finger into. And we were successful enough at it. Eventually it was standard procedure that Mick and I wrote songs for the Stones. After that Brian felt completely disillusioned. I think he felt this was a scene between Andrew, Mick, and me and he was being left out."

Ian Stewart also felt that Brian sensed he was being excluded:"Brian always felt a little left out of it . . . and he *was* left out because of his bloody stupidity. Because he used to do such dumb things; anything to upset people. Then he would get all pathetic—'nobody loves me' sort of thing. 'Why is everybody against me?'"

The more the pressure built, the *harder* the Stones worked. Brian would not sit down and tell Mick or Keith how he felt because, as Keith said, ". . . no one was in the condition to act in any rational or sane way. Incredible paranoias would start to come out. For instance, there was an incident backstage in this cinema, somewhere in the southwestern part of England. I had this chick in the dressing room. Brian was with Linda Lawrence at this point. Anyway, I was in a bad mood; hadn't slept or just got up.

Just before we went on stage we ordered in some food. I'd gone out of the room with this chick for about ten minutes and when I came back, Brian had eaten my piece of chicken! And so there we were with the announcer saying, 'Ladies and Gentlemen . . .the Rolling Stones . . .' Meanwhile, the chick's screaming, and Brian and I are in the dressing room with our guitars strapped around our necks, just thumping each other. I gave him this incredible black eye which lasted for about two months and went through these incredible colors from dark blue purple to green and yellow and got smaller and aged. All this because of a chicken leg."

Keith Richard admitted that before Andrew had him try songwriting, he thought it required a completely different talent. "Whereas the natural fact is that if someone puts their mind to it," he said, "and disciplines themselves, I'm sure they can write songs. Some blokes can write better than others; more prolific or in a certain style. But any musician who *really* wants to can write." Certainly, Brian was intelligent enough to compose and at that time he was playing excellent guitar and harmonica. Stew, however, described Brian as "incapable of writing music. Brian would be bitter because he couldn't write songs. But you can either write songs or you can't. And once you've written one you can churn them out by the dozens." Alexis came closer to the real issue when he said, "It was not strictly true to say that Brian couldn't write music, but his reticence in putting his music forward seems to be due to a mixture of shyness and lack of confidence."

In reality, Brian *did* try to write songs at home in Windsor. "I remember the beam of light that flashed on his face," Linda said, "when he wrote something he liked. Writing was a comfort to him. It was like talking to somebody. He was always writing poems and words for songs on

little pieces of paper. Obviously I loved them. They were romantic, sort of spiritual. His songs were like Donovan's —about his feelings. But Brian never said, 'I'll show the boys this one,' because he was insecure. He thought his things were too sentimental. I would encourage him to do his own things, but Brian would say, 'They're not finished,' That was his excuse all the time. And so he just kept to himself."

Brian's songs were his secret. (As I researched this book, I asked everyone if they had seen any of Brian's songs. Each person assured me that they had not, but named some other close friend who had certainly seen the songs. When I would meet and question these other friends, they would always supply me with a new name, but never a song.)

Alexis Korner, who was closest to Brian during his last months, said that although Brian was writing songs during that time, "he wouldn't show them to me. He'd only tell me about them. He always started out with a little bit about how he'd written songs which people wouldn't record. Then he'd start talking in vague terms about ideas he'd had for songs while staying in Morocco; things he wanted to get together. He would never come to terms about it. Brian would use the word 'song,' but at the end of two hours' conversation, you hadn't the slightest idea of what they were."

I asked Keith Richard if he had seen a song of Brian's. He said, "No, no. Absolutely not. That was the one thing he would *never* do. Brian wouldn't show them to anybody within the Stones."Peter Jones was one of the few people for whom Brian might have played his songs, but he didn't. "Brian had a terrible inferiority complex about songwriting," Peter said. "Early on, if you called up the Stones' office, Mick and Keith would immediately play you a tape. They'd get at it the quickest way possible. They wanted you to hear their work. But Brian was reluctant to let people hear his songs."

The only person Brian ever played his songs for was Linda. Yet he arranged the situation so that he could neither win nor lose: either Brian cared so much about someone's opinion that his fear of failure paralyzed him, or he deemed someone's opinion as lacking knowledge or insignificant. "When Brian played the songs he wrote," Linda said, "he didn't feel threatened by me. But that was just the trouble. I didn't matter at all."

Brian left some written pages with New York journalist Al Aronowitz. Aronowitz gave this song to Donovan for Brian's son, Julian:

(THANK YOU) For Being There??

1 As each sharp outline
      Melts and weaves
   And undulates in time
   With the compulsive

      rhythmic insistence
   Of each pounding musical line
   The scornful dancing lady dressed
   In black at last reveals
   She really isn't there at all
   She simply isn't real
   So thank you for being there
   —My love
   At least I know that you're real

2 As I speak with you of love
   —In metaphors and in code
   A need for satisfaction grows
   But they're stories still to be told
   Of experience and fantasies

Of vision and of fears
But when the visions fade
—you'll be there
Lying in my tears
Thank you for being there my love
Then I know that you're real

3 If the lashing tail of paranoiac fears
Strike my smarting face
Your understanding comforts me
And puts everything in its place
So shush, my love,
Your look and your touch
    can leave everything unsaid
And I can face all those
    little people
Just like Gulliver did.
Thank you for being there, my love
At last I've found someone who's real

4 The maniacal choirs that screamed out a warning
Now sings out lullaby
The walls that crashed to bury you and me
Now shelter our hideaway
Thank you for being there my love
At last I've found someone that's real
Thank you for being there my love
At last I know that you're real.

The more Brian felt left out of the Stones, the more he began to drink to excess. Linda worried about Brian's drinking, fearing for his already poor health, and they often fought about it. On one occasion, after Brian downed a bottle of liquor in an hour, Linda began crying and pleaded with him to stop. He screamed at her to quit nagging him and continued drinking.

As Brian grew moodier, and more withdrawn, Linda had trouble understanding him. Instead of realizing that other people and events, were also involved, Brian would often turn inward and blame himself for his unhappiness. He regarded himself as a chameleon who could change according to public whim, yet his inner constitution was stronger than he realized. His fears of not being what he wanted to be—a Mick Jagger—became more intense as the Stones gained popularity. Consequently, the fame and adoration only left Brian feeling more hollow.

Brian began seeing himself as evil and doomed. He wanted to shield Linda from his agony; he saw her feeling more helpless with him. Brian felt that he was being punished for something. He seemed to be protecting Linda from his problems by thinking, "You're too nice to have to go through what I have to go through."

During the latter part of 1964, Ellen Grehan interviewed Mick Jagger for the British TV program, *Ready, Steady, Go.* The program catered to teens with live appearances by rock stars and dancing teens. While Ellen interviewed Mick, her mother waited in a side room with Brian. After a four-hour interview Ellen and her mother went out for dinner. Ellen mentioned that, contrary to her expectations, and from her short conversation with him, Brian seemed a bright person. Her mother said that she had been moved by Brian's depression and sadness. Brian had told her that he felt the Stones were starting to shove him out of the group and without the Stones he would be nothing. He suspected they were not pleased with him.

"Brian just opened up to my mother," Ellen said, "maybe because she was an ordinary, down-to-earth Scottish housewife. Maybe because he felt that he *could* talk to her."

Brian suggested that he and Mrs. Grehan keep in touch and they went on to exchange three letters each. "My

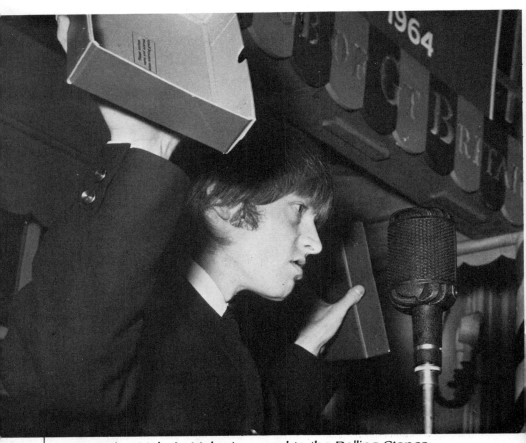

Accepting Melody Maker's *award to the Rolling Stones. October, 1964.*

mother told me," Ellen said, "that Brian's letters were very down. The hostility he felt from the other group members was very strong. He felt they were presenting a united front. But the saddest part was that he felt if he was no longer a Rolling Stone, then he was nothing: without that music there was no other reason for him to be."

During the mid-sixties, groups, not single performers, dominated the pop scene. For Brian to break from the Stones and try it alone would have been an extremely risky unprecedented move.

"Leaving the Stones would have been a big step down," Linda said. "Although Brian mentioned to me a couple of times that he was going to leave the group, he never actually did it. Brian went to Eric Clapton, who played with the

Yardbirds then, and said 'Maybe we could get something together' (which I thought would have been a good idea because they're both such sensitive people). I remember Brian asked Eric behind the Stones' backs, [and] it never came together because Eric stayed with the Yardbirds . . . but something held Brian to the Stones. I guess it was the beginning . . . the first thing he had created. And it's scary to go out on your own after having all that success. His music was his life, so he suffered through as much as he could."

Greil Marcus wrote in the memorial issue of *Rolling Stone* that featured Brian on the cover, "You can't come down from being a Rolling Stone. No way down, and one way out."

With Mick.

Leaving London for New York. June, 1966.

V

In 1965 the music scene was changing fast: Bob Dylan had his electric debut at the Newport Folk Festival; the Queen of England presented the Beatles with the Member of the British Empire award (MBE); the Rolling Stones released the single "I Can't Get No Satisfaction." It topped the charts in America and Britain—as did their album *Out of Our Heads*—and in thirty-seven other countries as well.

At the beginning of 1965 Brian lost a good friend, Cyril Davies. He had played harmonica in Alexis Korner's band and taught Brian how to play it. Friends gave a memorial concert for Cyril, featuring live music at the Flamingo Club in London. Here, Brian met Ronny Money, a petite Scotswoman. They became friends and remained close for the rest of Brian's life. Her bawdy wit, intelligence, and honesty attracted Brian.

"Brian was wandering about on his own looking lost," Ronny said. "I asked if he wanted a drink (in those days we used to carry our own bottles). Brian was shocked that someone spoke to him . . . he just sat watching a group performing. I asked him if he played—I didn't know who he was. He said, 'Yeah, I try to play the guitar.' He was extremely modest. And I thought, 'He's nice. I like him.' We chatted and watched the Eric Burdon set, which Brian liked."

A few hours later, back at Ronny's flat, Brian told her that he lived with his girlfriend Linda and her family. He said he loved them all and described Linda as "sweet."

Ronny, in turn, talked about her "old man, Zoot," who seems to have been a pretty outrageous character.

A month later Brian phoned Ronny and said he wanted to see her; he was in London for the evening. He came over and they chatted over tea, but Brian was still reserved when he talked about himself. Brian later told her that he "rarely met people who are friends of mine and don't want anything out of it, who don't want to bask in my limelight."

Brian was busy touring with the Stones but one night in February, 1965, he ran into Ronny at the Flamingo Club. The Rolling Stones had just returned from an Australian tour and were leaving for another performance the next morning. Brian invited Ronny back to his hotel room to spend the night. Once in the room, Ronny climbed into the unoccupied bed. Brian protested, "Where are you going? No, you're gonna sleep beside me."

"All right . . . but I tell you if you've got any ideas with me, forget it. I really don't want to know," Ronny said.

Brian petulantly stamped his feet: "Why don't you let me make it with you? Why don't you let me make it with you?"

Ronny, who was only 4'11", looked up at him, and mumbled, "Oh dear, I knew this was going to happen. All right, so I'm older than you. . . ."

Brian crawled on her bed and cuddled her, saying, "Now Ronny, own up. Come on, own up. Nobody will ever know."

"People will know . . . you and I know, and I've got a boyfriend (Zoot) somewhere out there in the great M1 drinking."

By this time the two of them had fallen on the floor laughing. Brian said, "Do you realize how many birds I've turned down in Australia? And you don't even think I'm good-looking, do you?"

Ronny burst out laughing.

"Neither do I, but it works," Brian said coquettishly, peeking out from behind his long hair.

The two spent the rest of the night jabbering, ordering room service.

Brian continued to visit Ronny whenever he had the time in London, and their chats grew longer and more intimate. Having a healthy nonsexual relationship was rare in their social group. Ronny described the people who congregated around the rock stars: "Those hangers-on don't know anybody because they never take the time to find out. They don't want to speak to anyone if they're down and everything's grey. They just say, 'That's a drag' and move on to someone who's up. Honesty to them is a thing they cannot handle under any circumstances. They don't want to know the truth. They don't want anybody to destroy the little illusions they have about the whole scene. Brian even told me, 'Whatever I am, whatever it amounts to (and it may amount to nothing), I can be it with you and I can be it with Linda.' And the tragedy was that he and Linda broke off."

Brian was weighed down by the reality of fatherhood, strained by the pressures of stardom and disappointed with the Stones' direction. New worlds had opened up to him; women, parties, excitement were easily available and all too tempting.

At the beginning of 1965, Brian and Linda decided not to live together. Linda stayed in Windsor and Brian found a flat in Belgravia. "Brian had to do his thing with the band," Linda said, "which was touring and making records. Brian thought the responsibility of Julian and I would just be too much. But I couldn't take it. The situation was so evil. Some rich boys who owned the Belgravia flat were the beginning of Brian's attracting people who wanted to hang out with him and get him drunk and stoned."

The breakup was agonizing to both of them. "After we had split up," Linda said, "I said I wanted to try it again. Brian said he didn't think so because he was going to die before he was thirty—so what was the point of getting it all together and blowing *my* mind anymore. Although he was emotional, he tried to put it very nicely, but I got the cold shivers; it was as if he had just seen a doctor and been told he had some terminal illness."

Ronny had her own version about the breakup. Brian visited Ronny frequently and told her about his feelings for Linda, how upset he was about what he had put her through. "He left Linda," Ronny said, "because he thought he was hurting her with the drug and star pressures. Brian became very unsure of himself and felt he was doing something better for Linda by leaving her. Brian had been with Linda for some very impressionable years. The pregnancy and the stardom—that's pretty heavy for a guy his age. So he moved out. Many new things were opening up to him and he got involved with a lot of things that hurt Linda. But I can say, and with some degree of authority, that Brian knew he lost the love of his life when he walked out on Linda. Linda was the only person he ever really loved because she was the only person who ever gave him anything for nothing. Linda was a shining light among all that shit."

Ronny continued, "Linda was in a lot of pain before they broke up. Brian was taking all sorts of amphetamines, which made him really paranoid. One night I made him stay at my place. I washed his hair for him to calm him down because he was in such a state. And I told him, 'Brian, you don't realize you're swallowing the pills like they were dolly mixtures, and they are not going to eliminate anything. Really, they're going to magnify everything. If you have to take something, smoke. At least it calms you to a certain degree. You don't need something to speed you up; you need something to slow you down.' "

In addition to taking speed, Brian started smoking marijuana. Brian would not let Linda get high. In fact, he would lock Linda out of the room when he smoked. "He kept trying to talk me out of all the things he was doing that he thought were bad," Linda said, "but he thought it was good for him. He needed it just to cope." At this time Brian told a friend, "No one would choose to live the kind of life I lead. Do you really think I enjoy it? But I mustn't complain or be bitter about it. It's brought the bread and the opportunity."

Brian's drinking also increased. Originally he only drank white wine, as all the Stones did, backstage before concerts. He then moved on to scotch and coke, or vodka and coke. By the end of 1964, Brian would return from the American tours with his private supply of alcohol in his

With Mick. Chicago, 1965.

flight bag. On those early tours, he wouldn't join in when the other boys were drinking, and at first, he wasn't suspected as being a closet drinker. Instead, he would go off with his TWA flight bag. He was secretive about the bag's contents and never opened it unless he was alone. "Brian got very heavily into drinking," Peter Jones said. "The point is that if somebody starts behaving strangely you can never really put your finger on what it is that's causing it. You don't see them doing anything but drinking, so you obviously tend to blame the drinking."

Brian began to drink openly. In pubs, where he would be instantly recognized, he went on binges. For a while, though, after Ronny turned Brian on to marijuana, he had episodes of almost religious temperance. In mid-1966 Brian dropped into a pub to visit Peter Jones and swore he would never drink again. With self-righteous morality he said, "I will leave you with your rotting livers. I will stick to my highs, you stick to yours. But yours are going to do you a lot more harm than mine." And to emphasize his point, someone was usually floating around the pub as a sober reminder of all that is wrong with having too much to drink.

A few months after the separation, in the summer of 1965, Linda went to Paris with several of Brian's friends, Robert Fraser and filmmakers Donald Cammell and Kenneth Anger. There she met Anita Pallenberg, who was soon to dominate Brian's life. "Donald and Kenneth knew Anita," Linda said. "She came over to visit and they introduced me to her thinking that we'd get on. Anita took me to this nightclub in Paris where we hung out for a while. She was very nice to me, gave me some clothes and some crazy pink tights. I thought, 'It's gonna be great hanging out with somebody who knows all these people.' When I was leaving to go back to England she said she was coming

With Anita Pallenberg, Heathrow Airport, December, 1966.

over there too, and maybe we could get a place together. I told her that I was still in love with Brian and rather than get involved with someone else I would like to do something on my own. Especially having Julian, I kept thinking that when you have a baby, you have to marry the father or keep him there for a while, just for the kid.''

Linda needed money to support Julian. In the past, Brian had given her money whenever she asked for it, but now he was more difficult about it. Linda finally decided that she would have to arrange the child support legally.

BRIAN JONES: 2 GIRLS IN A CASH FIGHT

By DON SHORT

TWO girls who had sons by ex-Rolling Stone Brian Jones are to claim a share of his fortune. ...eat-old hostel because we have no other money." Pat, a blonde, met Brian at a dance in their home town of Cheltenham nine years ago. "We set up home together and Brian stayed ...until Mark was had a model Linda Lawrence, 24, who has a five-year-old son, Julian. She and Julian were in California yesterday — but Linda's father, a Windsor builder, said: "Brian made a settlement of £1,000 at the time. "But this only paid for some bills he left behind, and all Linda got out of it for Julian was a cot and a pram and some clothes." It is believed that Jones, Stones last

"The word got out that Brian and I were going to write something up about child support," Linda said. "I had to give Brian's name and the papers blew it up saying, 'Oh, you're going to take him to court.' So I dropped the suit immediately. But if the press hadn't interfered, I probably would have gone through with it. They were going to make it sound so bad that it terrified Brian and I never sued.

"Linda would never ask Brian for anything," Ronny said. "It sounds like Linda knew him when he didn't have anything. Christ, so she did. These things happen. There's some people who *do* know you when you have nothing. But Linda wouldn't ask him for anything."

After Linda dropped the paternity suit, she and Brian went to Tangier together in September, 1965.

Brian visited Morocco many times and the country became a second homeland to him. No matter what befell him there, he was always lured back. He loved the accoutrements of Moroccan life and he would bring back caftans and Berber jewelry. (Al Aronowitz remarked that "Brian was the first heterosexual male to wear costume jewelry.") Brian was drawn by the intensity of the market places, the sensual foods eaten with the fingers, but most importantly, by the wild Moroccan rhythms of the steel drums and metal castanets. Brian would wander through the souks observing the musicians and trying to retain the musical flavor. When he saw an old Berber playing a reed or wooden instrument, Brian would try to capture a bit of the instrument itself. "Brian thought Morocco was amazing," Linda said. "He was into the exotic music which he heard in every restaurant we went to. He bought a variety of things in Morocco; the whole way of life seemed to attract him. Morocco was a place where he could forget all that had happened back in England."

But Brian and Linda's trip to Morocco was not really a reconciliation. Although the trip was an effort at trying to mend the tear in their relationship, it was no longer possible, there was no turning back. The feelings between the two during the trip were strained and distant. Brian's life was moving in a new direction and there wasn't room in it for Linda and Julian. Especially upsetting was that the press got wind of a story that Brian and Linda were going to get married; the reporters developed a small hurricane out of it. The couple suffered from the strain of fending off the publicity and the resulting ostracism from their friends Robert Fraser, Deborah Dixon and Donald Cammell, who had joined them in Morocco. Linda said, "After the press built up these stories, the people we were with acted coldly toward us. Brian felt freaked-out and paranoid. He felt he could never get away from the press and image. People pretend to be your friend and they play the game of *being* your friend. They are hangers-on. What confused me was that they were very nice; they give you things, take you into their homes, but if some trouble or some publicity comes up that is in bad taste, they turn off to you."

Brian returned to England early because of Rolling Stones' business. Linda, who returned with the others, carried—unbeknownst to her—some hashish through customs. "They said to me, 'Put this in your coat pocket,' " Linda said. "Robert Fraser gave me this thing, which turned out to be a huge lump of hash that I carried through customs. And I didn't know until afterwards what they had asked me to do."

Back in London, Linda saw Anita, Deborah, and Donald. Linda continued to live at home with her parents and Julian. "I kept wanting to make it," Linda said, "and keep all these things together emotionally. But these people just wanted to get stoned and have me freak out. I couldn't handle it."

Linda felt she could not stay in Windsor any longer and decided to move to America. Brian did give her some money for the move. "My reputation was completely gone," Linda said. "Having Julian was a big thing and I felt frightened, especially in this little town."

Brian never did find the nerve to tell his parents about his son, Julian. Mrs. Lawrence wrote to the Joneses to inform them of their new grandson. Mr. Jones' reply follows:

Ravenswood
335 Hatherley Rd.
Cheltenham
Glos.
19 . 3 . 65

Dear Mrs. Lawrence,

Many thanks for your letter which we received yesterday. Your news was, of course, most unwelcome, and we are sorry for your current anxieties.

We cannot say we are surprised or particularly shocked, as it seems that Brian and Linda have been living in considerably close association, and such an outcome seems eventually inevitable. It is nevertheless extremely regrettable.

However, many aspects of the situation seem very mysterious. You say the baby is nine months old, implying that it was born last June. We saw Linda twice in May, and we never had the slightest suspicion that birth was so imminent, or even to be expected at all. I spoke to Linda on June 1st and again at the end of June when Brian had come back from America. Nothing was said remotely suggestive of such an event.

Brian and Linda both stayed with us in October. Nothing in their conversation or manner aroused any suspicions.

You and Mr. Lawrence came to see us in January, and again no reference of any kind was made.

So after nine months of most successful secrecy, you have now told me, and I cannot quite understand why.

The threat of Press publicity is something that all of us would surely wish to avoid, as it could only prove to be a triple-edged sword, harming us all equally. If the secret has been kept so well for so long, I feel it could only become public if this were done deliberately, which I cannot feel anyone would wish.

Mr. Lawrence told me when you came that following a quarrel of some kind with Brian just before Christmas, Brian had left you. I cannot quite understand the timing of this, as I would have expected it to have taken place much earlier, if the baby was the prime cause, which I imagine it was.

Anyway, I repeat my regret, and my sympathies with you as Linda's parents, and with Linda herself. I do not forget Brian either, as his hard-won career is at stake, if the papers get hold of this story, or if anyone speaks out of turn. In such a case I have great fears for his actions as I know how terribly depressed and introspective he can be.

Finally, I pray that this unfortunate affair can be solved with no further hurt to any of the most concerned parties. It is one of the most mysterious episodes I have ever met with.

Yours sincerely,
Lewis B. Jones

Brian began seeing a woman named Zouzou toward the end of 1965. Zouzou, a French film star (who has since starred in *Chloe in the Afternoon*) knew very little English. She, like Anita Pallenberg, met Brian through mutual friends. Brian saw Zouzou regularly when in Paris and she stayed with him at his flat when she came to London. "Brian couldn't speak a word of French—or nearly nothing," Zouzou said. "It took such a long time to just say one thing to each other. He used to talk for hours and he'd get very mad because I couldn't understand. But he still was very, very nice."

"He was very scared of me. He always told me, 'You scare me to death.' "

"I said, 'Come on, Brian, I like you very much.' "

" 'Yes, but you don't love me. You don't think I'm beautiful.' "

"I thought he was really beautiful, but not to look at. But I think he was really somebody interesting. [But] more and more, everything was going wrong [for him]. He was crying nights because we couldn't *talk* to each other."

After the language barrier lessened, Brian and Zouzou discussed doing a film together. The story was about two people, a man and a woman, walking along opposite shores separated by a bridge. They meet on the bridge, very happy, looking into each other's eyes, falling in love. When they start to speak the girl speaks one language and the boy speaks another. They can't understand each other. Yet they try to make a life together eventually going off to live in a tower.

In a film made at this time on the Rolling Stones, *Charlie is My Darling*, Brian said, "I'm interested in making a film. I have a friend who has turned me on very much and the script is almost complete so I'll start working on that. I described it the other day as this new interpretation on the eternal theme of love, and it's really just that . . . I've just used two people in the film, a man and a woman. I want a third character to be 'love' which I'd try and project through the medium of the film, using sort of different techniques . . . images and symbols. It may not be a completely new, basic idea, but I'm sure that the way this is going to turn out will be very surrealistic . . . an abstract realism if you like."

Zouzou enjoyed Brian's company, his imagination and his enthusiasm about music. "I remember how glad he was when the Byrds came to visit him cause he loved them," Zouzou said. "About fifteen days before they came, he was telling me *every* day, 'They are coming in fifteen days. I'm going to meet them and they are the most fantastic people.' Everybody was beautiful. He loved people, really, but I think most of the people took him for a clown. They played with him and destroyed him."

"But he did so many beautiful things. One day when I was living in Paris, we went to a club and he was very drunk. I was really fed-up with him because he was too drunk and was smashing things. So I say, 'Okay, Brian, I'll meet you later at my place when you go to sleep, because I'm tired and I'm going to bed.' I was sleeping for about one hour and I heard Brian [come in], with flowers. And he said, 'That's for you, a present.' "

" 'That's very nice. Where did you get them?' "

" 'I found them.' "

" 'But at six o'clock in the morning? Where did you find them?' "

" 'I found them.' "

"The next day I found out that he stole the flowers from my concierge downstairs."

Another time he called her at 4:00 A.M. at her mother's house. Zouzou was in bed, and she told him, "I can't get up. I'm really sick."

He said, "Oh, I'll call you back later."

About ten minutes later he called her again. Zouzou said, "Oh, come on, Brian. I'm feeling bad and I want to sleep. You can call me tomorrow at 12:00."

He said, "Of course, of course. I'll call you tomorrow at 12:00."

In a few minutes Zouzou's doorbell rang. Her mother got up and found Brian standing there with an orange in his hand. He said, "I'm coming to give that to Zouzou. She's sick and oranges are good for her."

"He was trying really hard to understand," Zouzou remarked. "That was the most beautiful thing about him: he was not happy *because* he had money or things or was famous . . . he was trying to understand *why* he was famous, *why* he had money. This was really a big problem for him . . . I never met somebody who was so confused and wondering about himself—whether it was right or not to do this or that. Always questioning. He did not believe for one minute that he was right without putting a question first.

"He was always asking me for help—all the time. He was really trying very hard to come out. He was not like a devil trying to push people. He was getting depressed and asking me to help. After a few months, it was impossible for me to help him, to do anything for him. Because I told him one day, 'Brian, I don't know what's going to happen 'cause if I stay one more month with you I'd be in [a] mental hospital.' He was really going mad. I couldn't do anything for him and I was destroying myself because he was destroying himself.

"One night he started crying and I said, 'Why are you crying?' "

" 'You hate me.' "

" 'No, I don't hate you. Don't go on again with all those stories.' "

" 'You think I'm ugly.' "

"And he took a picture of himself and did all his face a different way. He said, 'Don't you think I'm much more beautiful like this?' "

"I said, 'No, you're much more beautiful than that.' "

"And he was getting all shaky and really out of his head. He called a hospital because he wanted to try and change his face. He was saying, 'You don't love me enough.' One day I find him in the bathroom and he's trying to cut his wrists. Or if he didn't do it, he was telling you that all the time. He hated himself. He felt he was a monster.

"I think he was obsessed because he always came back to that. We'd have three days really fantastic, everything fine. Then one night, you don't know why, he'd break down again for two days. And then three good days again. But at the end it was getting closer and closer. It was one hour fine and then break down."

Brian had a terrible inhibition about making love. He couldn't face it. He was too complicated, too inhibited. It was not whether it was good or not—he was not making love at all, because most of the time he was too stoned. But it was really something terrible for him to be in love with a girl and not be able to touch her. One day he told Zouzou that he would "dirty" her if he touched her. "I tried to help him by being kind to him," Zouzou said, "and not pointing out this problem. I was thinking if we just forget it one night, if it doesn't happen, write it off. The next day it won't be a problem for him. So we didn't talk about it."

"He was feeling very, very depressed and starting to have big bags under his eyes, drinking a lot. We decided to go to Marrakesh together. The day before we left, some friends of mine came over and said, 'You shouldn't go with him to Marrakesh because it's really the same thing over there.' So I stayed in London and he went to Marrakesh. Brian said to me, 'When I come back I'm going to be feeling very well. I'm going to lay in the sun and be healthy.' But when he came back he was just like before, nothing changed. He was very white with big bags under his eyes."

In August 1965, the Stones' "Satisfaction" hit all over the world. Brian had very little to do with the record; he only played rhythm guitar. Purely a Mick and Keith venture, its astounding success only made Brian feel more isolated. This record marked another turning point for Brian. He became aware that the Rolling Stones could carry on perfectly well, if not magnificently, without him, and that he was no longer irreplaceable.

Around this time, Anita Pallenberg phoned Brian, reintroduced herself and invited herself over to Brian's apartment. Brian, who was very stoned, said, "Sure, yeah, . . . come on over." Anita held a very strong attraction for Brian. Linda remembers that time in 1965 when she felt that "the world and everything is such a mess, why not get stoned and hang out with these crazy people who have all these comfortable things? They were so flash. They had all these beautiful and lovely things that attracted you, things that you wanted to have too. You just came from a normal family. The beauty of it all attracted Brian. Anita was just coming into wanting to be an actress. I remember conversations in Paris when they were trying to encourage me to be a part of their scene; you get people like Donovan, who have money on their own, you enter their lives—that was the attitude I got from them. They were models and movie stars and script writers, but they needed a backing and a name. They were looking for that kind of connection."

Ronny elaborated: "Brian threw himself in at the deep end. At that particular time he was out for as many kicks as he could get. Anita was great. She excited Brian—whatever young guys only read about he was getting on a plate. She was into the bisexual number and arranged scenes. Brian figured, 'Right. This is what it's all about. This is what people want of me. . . .' Because Brian didn't know. I kept saying, 'What do *you* want?' He'd just say that he didn't know. Brian could be easily put upon if a person exerted certain emotional pressures. Female fans couldn't exert any pressure because they were overawed by him. But when you *could* take or leave Brian, the star (which was basically what he wasn't into), the minute you could sort of shrug your shoulder about it, he saw a ray of hope— as if to say, 'At least this person is accepting me for me. A fan wouldn't just take me or leave me.' "

Keith, who was with Anita for over ten years, said, "Anita's incredibly strong. A much stronger personality than Brian's, more confident with no reservations, whereas Brian's was full of doubts." Jo Bergman, long-time secretary and confidante to the Stones, described Anita as "fearless." Even a shopkeeper who used to wait on Brian said, "Brian was ruled by Anita to a large degree." Christopher Gibbs, long-time friend of Brian, Mick, and Keith, described Anita as a ". . . pretty powerful sort of person. She'd been exposed to many more different kinds of life than Brian. And Brian, being primarily a music person (to the exclusion of a lot other things), probably relied on

Anita for stimulation and information, tuning him in on things he didn't know about."

The Stones toured America during the last months of 1965. Brian was hospitalized in Chicago for a drug overdose, and missed several gigs. Obviously the pressure was on. But, Anita flew to Hollywood to join Brian, and told the press: "If he asks me to marry him I shall. We may get married in the States. I am very much in love."

At the same time, Linda was living in Los Angeles and through mutual friends, ran into Brian. "Lawyers used to come up to me saying, 'When Brian comes into town we

On stage with Mick on their first American tour. Cleveland, 1964.

can get you some money because you shouldn't have to look after Julian.' I was really struggling. Anyway, we saw each other at Alan Pariser's house. Brian knew I was in America and wasn't surprised at all. He seemed upset that Anita might get mad because I was there. When I went up to speak to him, he was cold and there was no communication. But I kept thinking, 'Brian's got to go through certain things and I'm going to wait.' " In an interview right after Brian's death, Linda said, "I was always in love with Brian. Even when he went out with other girls I never gave up hope that one day he would eventually come back to me."

Ladies and Gentlemen . . . THE ROLLING STONES. 1966.

VI

1966: that was the year when London was "Swinging"; John Lennon declared that the Beatles were more popular than Jesus; LSD came under federal regulation in the U.S.; Bob Dylan had a motorcycle accident and went into seclusion; and *TIME* magazine featured "Is God Dead?" on their cover.

As Donovan described the sixties: "It was romantic. You left home and went to other towns. People would look at you and say, 'Who are you? You're a wild man with long hair and jeans.' There weren't very many long-haired people around. The whole movement was so exciting because it was localized everywhere, but sustained by a collective thought, a *musical* thought. The charts rang with this sound, this freedom tone, this steaming rock 'n' roll. The strain in the fifties produced the sixties; digging the old beatnik tradition of discussing art and radical things. There was no strain in the sixties, just bleedin' chaos and expression. What can you build on that? Mary Quant was freakin' out in London and the whole fashion world followed her. Most of us who went through the sixties only became aware of our position in the last two or three years. After the sixties fell, the whole generation involved in the revolution was disillusioned. Before that, the events were too crazy and everybody was too busy rushing over each other."

New clubs mushroomed while old clubs changed hands, and the scene gathered momentum with the fast tempo of the times. Young Londoners dropped in at clubs and sampled the strobe-lit music nightly. Brian hung out at a club called "Blases" (in Kensington, just north of Chelsea) about three nights a week. Jim Carter-Fae, the manager of Blases, as well as the Pheasantry Club and later the Speakeasy, was on a constant lookout for new talent. He regularly featured English bands (Marmalade, Traffic, Family) and whenever an American band came to England he tried to book them. The Byrds, the first American group to play at Blases, were soon followed by the Lovin' Spoonful, Otis Redding, Paul Butterfield, and the seventeen-person Ike and Tina Turner Revue, which performed on a stage no wider than fifteen feet. Later, when the club started featuring soul music, Jim booked Wilson Pickett and Chuck Berry. Even Ravi Shankar played his only club date at Blases one night in 1966. People in the pop business frequented the club: models, photographers, musicians, filmmakers, as well as advertisers, stockbrokers, and bankers.

Whenever Jim booked someone special like Ike and Tina Turner or the Byrds, the Beatles and the Stones showed up. They also gave a party for Dylan at the club. Jim said, "It was a great party. Dylan was out of his head. He was just carried in and carried out."

It came as a surprise to many that Brian was involved and productive in the recording of *Aftermath* after his lack of interest in the Stones' post-"Satisfaction" music.

The band worked hard on this music and some said Brian made his greatest musical contribution to this album. He wove odd bits of classical and ethnic sounds into the fabric of rock 'n' roll. It was a novel approach. "The studio at RCA in Hollywood was loaded with every instrument under the sun, and the instruments would be lying around from other sessions," Keith said. "Brian would learn enough about an instrument, sometimes only for one song, to play what he wanted. This was his greatest gift. He would wander from instrument to instrument on each tape. The actual fact is that he played very little guitar after the first couple of records. I used to overdub nearly all of them, although it's not true of every track, obviously. Brian was one of those people who could pick up any instrument and bring something nice out of it, even though he'd never played it before." Peter Jones said, "Keith was a more natural guitarist, but Brian had a wider field of vision. Brian was a better all-around musician."

Listen to "Paint It Black" for a great example of Brian's genius. The sitar, as lead instrument, dominates the song's tone. Keith called Brian's sitar work on that song "amazing."

David Dalton, in his book *The Rolling Stones: The First Twenty Years,* had this to say: "Brian's attack on the sitar was innovative. His playing was more percussive than melodic, sharper and more treble, exploiting its tonal range in a way George Harrison's respectful treatment did not begin to explore. Brian's innovation was to integrate the sitar into the total sound of "Paint It Black." He gave the sitar a rock inflection with a shrill, metallic, twangy timbre that was closer to an electric guitar than to an exotic stringed instrument. There is nothing remotely quaint in Brian's exploitation of the sitar as a rock device; it fit naturally into the sound with the ease the Hawaiian guitar incorporated as pedal steel into country music or of eccentric Caribbean tunings adopted by Delta blues."

On "Lady Jane" Brian's harpsichord and dulcimer set the song's Elizabethan tone. They perfectly reflected the song's content. At that time no one else in England used the dulcimer in rock compositions.

Brian played marimbas on "Under My Thumb" and harpsichord on "I Am Waiting." But the tour de force was Brian's harmonica on "Goin' Home," which pointed a new direction for harpists.

During the *Aftermath* recording sessions, Brian sometimes participated. Yet other times he appeared totally unconcerned which bewildered the other band members. "After about the third year, Brian was very disinterested in the music," Keith said, "because having to play Jagger-Richard compositions bruised his ego. Brian felt the Stones weren't playing the music they should be, which was the music he started off playing with [them]. Though, in fact, Brian was the first one to try and change the Stones' music when he suddenly had that big Beatles thing. He was conflicted about it. At the *Aftermath* sessions, Brian would be down on his back, lying around in the studio with his guitar strapped around him, and the record would be made around him. Then other times he would contribute amazing things. Suddenly, from nine hours of lying there, (or often not being at the sessions at all for two or three days which would really get up everybody else's back), he'd just walk into the studio and lay some beautiful thing down on a track (piano, harpsichord), something that nobody'd even thought of. The number of instruments he played was countless; you couldn't put a number on it. He could get enough out of an instrument, almost any instrument, including harp, which is one of the most difficult to play, for one particular song. He could just sit down, figure it out, and play it. There was no limit." Keith was referring to Brian's harp-playing on the song "On With the Show" which appeared on *Their Satanic Majesties Request.*

Brian told journalist Sue Mautner: "I've always been more interested in musical instruments than the others, because I'm an instrumentalist. Do you know, I don't know the words of most of our songs. That's why I play the piano, sax and clarinet—because I don't sing!"

Glyn Johns remembered a time when Brian came to a session with a child's ukulele—the kind sold in dime stores. No one Glyn knew of could even *tune* the thing, not to mention play it. But Brian, within the space of an hour, was not only playing it, but getting melodies out of it.

"Sometimes Brian would be really turned on at the end of a session," Keith said, "which really made us feel good, because usually Brian felt bad. He was against what was happening, but he was also all for it. He was against being second fiddle to Mick and me, especially Mick. (Being second to me because I was writing the stuff.) Yet Brian loved being a pop star probably more than Mick and I ever have. He loved to be adored, and was very agreeable with anyone who did it, even though it means nothing."

Stew had a different point of view about Brian's musical contributions. He saw Brian more as a dilettante: "Whereas Mick and Keith lived together—they wrote, practiced, and played—Brian didn't bother. He was getting terribly interested in instruments other than the guitar and he dabbled quite happily. He enjoyed picking up these other instruments and learning to do bits and pieces on them. And it got to the state where he didn't want to play guitar at all. The only thing he *wanted* to do was to have Keith and Bill and Charlie and whoever was playing piano put down a track (and then if Keith wanted to add another guitar, fine), and Brian would overdub his dulcimer, et cetera. That is 100 percent true because they would start playing a song, Keith and Brian playing guitar, then Brian would get fed up with it, say he wasn't getting the sound he wanted or his guitar was broken or this, that, or the other or his fingers were hurting. They hurt because he never bothered to play as much as he had to so, of course, his fingers would hurt."

This ambivalence was ripping Brian apart. He wanted to be part of the Rolling Stones and at the same time he loathed it. He hated playing Mick and Keith's music; he was jealous of them and at the same time, he looked down on them as though they had lost the true spirit of the music. Yet Brian wasn't strong enough to leave the group because he was afraid he would be nothing without them.

Brian became friendly with Bob Dylan during the early U.S. tours. Some say the song "Ballad of a Thin Man" (with the refrain referring to "Mr. Jones") was especially written for Brian. In fact, a letter written to *Rolling Stone Monthly* by some American fans quoted Dylan, at the Carnegie Hall concert in 1965, as saying: "This ["Like a Rolling Stone"] is written for Mr. Jones. The other ["Thin Man"] was about Mr. Jones. This is for him."

Al Aronowitz, friend of both Dylan and Brian, said, "Brian was crazy about Dylan and Dylan liked Brian." Keith said, "[Brian] was the only one of us who hung out with Dylan for a bit." Dylan would greet Brian by saying, "How's your paranoia?" By this time Brian had developed a distinctive harmonica playing style, yet on the song "Who's Been Sleeping Here?" from the *Between the Buttons* album, Brian abandons his style and copies Dylan's.

In rehearsal for Beggar's Banquet. 1968.

Brian also displayed his eclectic instrumental skills on *Between the Buttons*. On "Ruby Tuesday" Brian played recorder and cello, once again lending gentleness to the Stones' otherwise harsh compositions. He played banjo and kazoo on "Cool, Calm, and Collected," marimbas and harpsichord on "Yesterday's Papers," and a comical trombone on "Something Happened to Me Yesterday."

In 1966, the Rolling Stones toured Australia and New Zealand in February and March, five European countries in March and April, North America in June and July, and Great Britain in September and October. They also released four albums: *High Tide and Green Grass* (a "best-of" album) *Aftermath, Got Live if You Want It* (live) and *Between the Buttons*.

During the tour in the summer of 1966, Brian collapsed. People who worked and traveled with the band on the tour gave Brian (or anyone else who wanted them) every conceivable drug available. Brian sampled everything until he was hospitalized. The press was told he had pneumonia. But the group tension contributed to Brian's desperation more than anything, including the drugs. And he felt worse when the Stones continued their tour, went on to Hollywood and began to record an album at RCA studios, without him.

"We did the mid-west dates without Brian," Keith said. "That drove me frantic because I had two guitar parts. I mean it was hard work for a band that was slowed down to making do with only one guitar. It was a drag. And Brian didn't care; he wanted to be in the hospital. At that time Mick and I were incredibly cruel to Brian. But when you've been on the road three or four years, you tend to get very cruel, especially toward your friends—crueler than to anybody else. I used to do this vicious imitation of Brian. It was all funny, but incredibly cruel, and people used to just roll up laughing."

"It was a period that was really bitter, very nasty (not for Mick and I particularly, but for Brian). Mick and I were really confident and thought we were doing exactly what we wanted to do. Brian didn't appear to want to participate: he didn't give a damn whether he did or not. Brian knew what records we wanted to make and how we wanted them to sound and if he didn't want to put anything into it, we really didn't care. We knew what we wanted to do anyway. Of course, this only hurt him more, but it wasn't to be stopped in 1966."

It was then that something broke inside Brian Jones that was never to be mended. Music was Brian's great love, and he expressed that love through the Rolling Stones, but the music they were making ceased to mean much to him. Brian detached himself from the group, playing halfheartedly, but passionless performances debilitated him. He craved the intensity he had felt in the early days. In many ways he became a mere ornament in the band. To fall from the position of leader to nothing more than a glittering appendage was a tremendous blow to his self-esteem. Brian could not adjust to this diminishing power, this role as "employee." The loss was too great.

Yet it seemed as though there was no way out. At that time there were very few solo rock stars; most were in groups. Moreover, Brian was not a disciplined songwriter. Although his ideas were profound and innovative, he knew he couldn't write music that could compete with Jagger-Richard compositions. But then again, did he really want to compete with them or did he want to return to the blues? Brian chose the easy route. Better to just continue, get stoned and try not to feel the pain.

"In 1966," Keith said, "after we recorded *Between the Buttons*, I realized exactly what had gone down when we were touring that last year. A lot of what happened you can analyze or write that I was suffering from this, that, or the other, but actually it was just the road pressures. You don't realize them when you're going through it. You think, 'I'm going crazy. He's going crazy.' These tiny things blow up into enormous problems. But as soon as the pressure came off I found that I could be with Brian just like I was before the Stones were anything to anybody. After that last tour in '66, Mick suddenly went to Australia with Marianne—doing this huge courtship job on her—taking her off on yachts. So Brian knew I wasn't having any contact with Mick. That barrier was immediately wiped out because he knew I was on my own. . . . The triangular flow of energy between Brian, Mick, and myself was the thing the Stones ran on. It was this conflict and interchange of allegiances which was the basic emotional engine of the Stones . . . Brian knew I wasn't seeing Mick and sayin' 'Oh, Brian's doin' this' . . . or 'Oh, Brian's been smoking this or taking that or trying. . . .' He knew I wasn't putting him down behind his back—that the other third of that triangle wasn't in play at that particular point. So he knew that whatever was going down was for real. Brian and I had a great time together. He was a really great friend—terrific to hang out with if he wasn't feeling paranoia toward you."

"We had only one album for the next year and no real tours, so I found myself back in London with nothing to do. I went over to Brian's new place a lot mainly because on this last tour we'd all started really blowing a lot of grass, freakin' out, getting high—getting into a relationship with him which I hadn't had for nearly two years, like it was all forgotten—almost. And I had no ulterior motive for going around there except that was where everyone was hanging out. . . ."

It was about this time that Brian began to heavily experiment with fashion. He had moved to an apartment with Anita on Courtfield Road near the Gloucester Hotel. Details of the apartment charmed Brian, like the abundance of carved wood, an immense studio with a thirty-foot ceiling and wraparound windows, the trap door in the kitchen hiding steps which led to a wine cellar, and a gallery bedroom tucked above the studio, accesible only by rope ladder.

Beautiful bits of cloth poured out of every drawer, every cupboard in Brian's flat. Brian chose his daily dress like an artist constructing a collage. He was the first rock star to encircle his knees as well as his neck with scarves. He decorated himself with Berber necklaces and bracelets, and antique brooches, bits of old textiles, brocades and silks. They linked him to another time and place. "He was the first man I ever knew," Al Aronowitz said, "to wear costume jewelry bought in the ladies department at Saks. He set the style in many ways. He was the prototype of the English pop star."

Brian could turn his clothing into a brilliant personal statement. As Alison Lurie said of people like Brian in *The Language of Clothes:* "Between cliché and madness in the language of dress are all the known varieties of speech: wit, information, irony, propaganda, humor, pathos and even (though rarely) true poetry. Just as a gifted writer combines unexpected words and images, risking (and sometimes briefly gaining) the reputation of being deranged, so certain gifted persons have been able to combine odd items of clothing, old and new, native and foreign, into a brilliant eloquence of personal statement. While other people merely follow the style of the age in which they live, these men and women transform contemporary fashion into individual expression."

If Brian followed anything through to its end, it was dressing gypsy-fashion. When he attended the Monterey Pop Festival during the summer of 1967 (he stayed with Sheila Oldham, Andrew's wife, and Nico, the lead singer of the Velvet Underground), he brought a trunk full of

The quintessential Brian Jones: flamboyant, bold, and unorthodox.

clothes. Every day he would try on scores of outfits and ask the women's opinion. After several assemblages, Nico urged Brian to stop. But Sheila encouraged him: "Put more clothes on, Brian. Load them on."

Clothing for Brian, much like it is for many women, was his strongest mode of self-expression. Everything was coordinated for a beautiful effect. He proved that a man could wear outrageous, even feminine clothes and still look attractive and masculine. His sense of style blurred the edges between men and women. Not only were pop stars following his lead but the record buying public and hippies as well.

Robert Fraser, Michael Cooper (the Stones' photographer), Christopher Gibbs and Tara Brown (who died soon after in a car accident which the Beatles sang about in "Day in the Life") hung out at Brian's Courtfield flat. A decade later, Keith told me about this time in 1966: "Everyone was hanging out at Brian's flat and people were learning from each other for the first time in years. Instead of just sitting on each other's shoulders in hotel rooms, we were talking to a lot of other people like Robert Fraser, who was running an art gallery. And Christopher Gibbs, who owned an antique shop, was turning Brian on to a lot of things." Brian spent much of his time with this new circle of friends, especially Gibbs.

Christopher, Brian, and Anita decided to take a trip to Tangier together. They chose to stay at the Minzah Hotel in a large suite overlooking the sea. About ten minutes after the trio arrived, Brian and Anita began fighting violently. Brian raised his hand to strike Anita and missed, slamming his arm on an iron window frame, breaking his wrist. (This incident has been referred to in other sources as a "climbing accident.") Christopher and Anita took him to La Clinique Californie, where he remained for several days. In the meantime, Anita and Christopher explored

Tangier, and one day ran into a mysterious-looking man near the flower market, holding a white Chinese vase and a small leather pouch in his hands. He approached them, introduced himself as Ahmed, and whispered, "Would you like to have a smoke?" Anita and Christopher followed him at breakneck speed as he wound in and out of the market. He finally led them up a stone staircase, behind the Minzah, to an empty shop. Hidden in a corner was a small leather bag containing hash and Berber jewelry. There, Christopher and Anita smoked great quantities of hash. As soon as Brian's arm was set and plastered, they took him to Ahmed's. Brian kept saying, "Got to get some of this gear back to London." Ahmed hid half a kilo of hash in the bases of two brass candlesticks. Brian paid for the dope but had Christopher take the risk of sending it over: "Man, you've got this antique shop. There won't be any problem; they'll think it's for your shop." The candlesticks arrived safe and the trio ceremoniously unsoldered the bases.

In the evenings in Tangier, Brian, Christopher, and Anita would go down to the Medina to sip cups of mint tea, smoke a lot of good dope, and look through tons of things, squabbling good-naturedly about who was going to buy them. It was exciting to find fabric that had been stacked up in dusty corners since the war— unusual embroideries done by Jews in Tetuan.

Brian spent much of his time in Morocco listening to the musicians. "Brian was so interested in music," Christopher said, "and musical instruments and sound, that if he saw an old beggar sitting on the floor playing some particular reed or flute, despite that fact that he was incredibly shy, deeply paranoid, and couldn't speak French or Arabic particularly well, he would somehow manage to communicate his deep and serious interest in what the musician was doing by making sound come out of his bit of wood. And it used to be very nice to walk through a crowded African city with Brian and he would do this and it would be delightful.

"Brian was one of those people who could shut himself off from any exterior influences when he was trying to work out how to play a new instrument. I think music of any kind was the one thing that Brian always responded to. Hearing a flute in a marketplace or anyone beating on a drum, he'd instantly respond. If he saw a peculiar instrument in a store or junk shop, he'd always have to try to make it work. And [he'd] get right into it, completely forgetting about anything else that might be bothering him. He was a real musician, one completely in tune with that side of things."

The trio returned to London and life resumed its roller-coaster course. A coterie of hangers-on formed around Brian. He would usually allow them easy access to his possessions, just to secure their companionship. He was used by many people who gave nothing back to him—emotionally or intellectually. When these "friends" went home after having a good evening with Brian Jones, the star, in a restaurant where Brian paid the bill, he was left alone, feeling completely drained, knowing full-well the whole thing would be repeated the next day. Brian simply didn't have the self-discipline to end it. As a friend mentioned, "Brian was so afraid of not being liked he laid out any amount of money to be liked."

Brian's friend Ronny and Anita had first met down at the Scotch St. James Club a year earlier. The women responded strongly to each other. "I went down to Scotch's one night when everybody happened to be there," Ronny said. "I was talking to Jimi Hendrix and Eric Burden (and I hadn't seen Brian for some time). I noticed Brian through a crowd of people. He saw me and ran up screaming, 'Ronny! Ronny!' and started hugging me. He said to Anita, 'This is

Ronny . . .' and all of that. Anita said words to the effect of 'Is this another one of your sleeparounds? I thought I'd met most of them,'—which I didn't take too kindly to, but I figured I'm older than those people. But Brian (and I had never seen him do that before) shot over and punched her in the nose. Anita's nose was bleeding and everybody was looking when he said, 'Don't you dare talk about her like that.' Anita just stood there with a gob full of blood. Afterwards she played it very cleverly; she decided I wasn't too bad."

Many inflamed arguments punctuated Brian and Anita's relationship. Brian once confided to Ronny that he thought Anita was like a huge sponge that drained everything out him. "Anita didn't allow Brian any time to rest," Ronny said. "She was all me me me. Nobody could live around that. A lot of people can get boundless energy when they shove amphetamines down their faces all day."

Brian often could not cope with what his life was becoming. A few weeks after the party incident with Ronny and Anita, he told Ronny he would pay her to live with him—not as a lover, but to protect him from the people he was too weak to turn away. Ronny told Brian that he had to learn to trust himself, that he could not count on always having someone around him. "I don't think Brian could face whatever it was that he'd become," Ronny said. "And when you're on your own you *have* to face it. I think he got near to it when he was with Linda. "

A few days after asking Ronny to live with him, Brian phoned her at work, begging her to come over to his flat. "And that place . . . ." Ronny said, "It was completely disgusting. Brian was in a terrible state. He was crying—mind you, at that particular time he was back taking speed and all sorts of methadrine. Brian said, 'Can you get me a girl?' Let's face it, coming from him . . . a Rolling Stone . . . and all you read about their women. . . . I said, 'What are you talking about? What do you want? Do you want to go to bed with her?'

" 'I just want somebody that's gonna be with me, even if I've got to pay the money. At least I know they're there because I'm paying them. I *know* it's because of the money. I don't know whether people want to be with me because I'm me or 'cause I'm Brian Jones of the Rolling Stones.' "

"It upset me so. . . . And as a matter of fact I found a girl and told her, 'A friend of mine wants a girl. I don't think he particularly wants to go to bed; I think he wants someone to be there with him, but you'll get paid.' The girl spent the night with Brian and called me the next day and said, 'He was so nice. All he wanted to do was talk and I cuddled him a little.' "

On February 6, 1967, the Stones performed on the prestigious television program, *Sunday Night at the London Palladium.* The day before the show, Brian, Anita, and Keith went shopping at a Chelsea clothing store, "Granny Takes a Trip." At Granny's, Brian ran into an old friend, Tony King, who was working as a publicist for Apple Records. Keith wore a "Jesus Saves" teeshirt and Brian, festooned with jewelry, wore five or six layers of clothing with scarves tied around his knees and elbows. Brian asked Tony if he liked his shirt.

"It's marvelous," Tony said, in reference to Brian's outermost garment.

"No, not that one . . . this one . . . ." Brian reached down around his neck, and fished out a bit of shirt that had been buried from view, yanked it forward for inspection.

The following night, when the Rolling Stones played on the television show, Brian and Keith wore the same outfits that they had worn at Granny's. They had not even bothered to change for this important performance.

For the show's finale, it was a custom for all the performers to stand on the revolving stage and wave goodbye. Even though this finale was the show's trademark, the Stones refused to participate, causing a scandal in the press. Brian ran into Peter Jones shortly thereafter and they talked about the incident. Brian told him, "Mick and Keith thought we were going to lose our reputation by getting on the revolving stage—because it's show biz schmaltz. But, quite honestly, I don't agree. The Stones will probably sell a hundred thousand records as a result of being on this type [of] television program. I didn't see why we didn't just do what the others did."

There were more pressing problems at the end of February 1967. Mick, Keith, Christopher Gibbs, Marianne Faithfull, and Robert Fraser were busted at Keith's country house. The Stones felt they had been set-up. "Originally the only person who got charged was myself," Keith said, "because it was my house. Mick had a few pills, amphetamines which you could buy across the counter in Italy, but were illegal in England. The Prime Minister could walk into a chemist in Milan and say, 'I must stay awake, could you give me a couple mild No-Doz?' And then find that he could be busted here in England for two or three months. What eventually happened was the authorities went too damn far—like giving me a year for allowing people to smoke dope in my house. Not that they ever proved it. It was never brought up whether I'd smoked dope in my house or if I'd even known it was going on.

"This bust was the beginning of the end for Brian. Brian and Anita were supposed to come down to my place for that weekend, but at the last minute they couldn't make it. They just couldn't get it together and get down to the country because there weren't any right roads. They'd called up and said they weren't coming. (George Harrison was there with Patti. He'd been gone no more than half an hour before the cops arrived, which makes my mother like him. It would have been interesting to see what would have happened if they'd caught him there. Then again maybe they were waiting for George to go.) Anyway, what happened was that they took away all those so-called substances from my house.

"Everybody felt, 'Oh, what a bring-down. Let's all go to Morocco, take a load off, and cheer up.' And this is what everybody did. Me, Brian, Anita, and Deborah Dixon decided to drive down in my Bentley. At this time Brian and Anita weren't getting along. They had reached an impasse about Anita's movie career. Brian resented it for some reason. She was working on the German film *A Degree of Murder* and Brian was writing the music for it. Brian wanted to be, to a certain extent, the star of the relationship and for Anita to be this chick with a star. It was getting on her.

"We were driving through France on the way to Morocco and Brian fell sick. Whereas everybody else was buzzing on this incredible high, Brian was going his other way. I think it was genuinely directed at calling for Anita's attention or something. It was just such a weird trip over the Pyrenees into Spain. Brian got this terror of mountains. It was an asthmatic thing, which is all psychosomatic and mixed up with the head thing. After he collapsed we stayed a couple of days with him to see how he was getting on. Then the doctors said, 'Oh, yes . . . he's in a bad way. He'll be here a week.' We said, 'Oh . . . um . . . this, that, and the other . . . we'd better go.' But damn it, after all trust him.''

Deborah, Keith, and Anita continued their trip to Tangier. This was Keith's first time in Morocco and Anita showed him around. According to Keith this was when he and Anita began their affair. After about a week, Anita and Deborah went back for Brian and brought him to Morocco.

Keith deplored Brian's behavior, especially when Brian began coming on to Moroccan women. "Things eventually blew up once and for all when I took Anita out of Marrakesh," Keith said. "I couldn't sit by and watch the way Brian was treating Anita although she was well capable of looking after herself. It wasn't some Sir Galahad number. It's just that it wasn't worth it—'Why don't you get out?' It was a very cold-blooded affair. We arranged for somebody to take him off and listen to some Moroccan musicians—long enough for us to spring out of town with him hot on our tracks."

Brion Gysin, who spent the afternoon with Brian while Keith and Anita were making their escape, described in *Moroccan Mishaps with the Strolling Ruins* how Brian's driver Tom Keylock arranged the afternoon. " . . . I run into Tom with a message. Tom comes on strong like a Stone. . . . Right now a small plane has just landed in Marrakesh chockablock full of reporters come down to persecute us. The Stones are strong. The Stones will win but we do have one weak link. You know who it is, Brian. Brian talks 'is bloody head off to reporters. . . . Brian must be kept away from them for his own good. And ours. . . . Why don't you take him out recording live music on this great public square like you said you would. Bring him back about six or a bit after."

When Brian returned to his room at the Minzah Hotel he found that Anita, Keith, and everyone else had left. He searched the room frantically for a note, some word or explanation. Nothing. He ran down to the main desk asking "Is there any note for me? Did my friends leave any forwarding address?" Nothing. He dashed back up to the room sobbing and yelling at the same time. He called everyone he could think of. But there was no news about where Anita and Keith had gone—and nothing would ever bring them back.

"Anita dug Brian a lot, very much." Keith said years later, "A lot of things she hated. Sometimes I remember Anita saying it was what Mick and I done to him that made him not well, because Anita and I talked about Brian a lot. Mick and I really didn't do anything to Brian that was avoidable in any way—because there was no time to sit back and think about what we were doing. Everything was done on impulse and instinct. There was no trying to intellectualize and rationalize about it or analyze it. Things just happened. It was a fascinating period. Nobody was attached to anybody. Nobody had families or anything to consider. I know a lot of people blame me and Anita for that thing . . . Brian's father. . . ."

When Keith mentioned Brian's father blaming Anita and him for Brian's death, he was referring to a radio program called *The Story of Our Time.* On that show, Lewis Jones said, "What I firmly believe was that when he lost the only girl he ever loved, this was a very severe blow to him. He changed suddenly and alarmingly—from a bright enthusiastic young man to a quiet and morose and inward-looking young man. So much so—when his mother and I saw him for the first time for some months after this happened, we were quite shocked by the change in his appearance and in my opinion, he was never the same boy again. And it was at that time I believe that he got mixed up with drugs, if indeed he was. Whether he just took to drugs in the way many people take to drink. . . . I don't know. I shall never know. I am convinced and always shall be convinced that was the turning point in Brian's life, rather than the pop scene generally."

However, Christopher Gibbs, a close friend of Brian's at the time said, "Those who attribute all of Brian's happiness to Anita don't know anything about it. I never thought Brian was happy with whoever he was with, but he was just happy according to how the music was going."

Upon his arrival back in London, Brian called Ronny. "Brian told me," Ronny said, "that Anita fucked off and left him in Marrakesh, semi-conscious I might add. She just left, because Brian was on the way out and Keith was on the way in. . . ."

The act of Anita leaving Brian for Keith was doubly devastating. On the one hand was the callous manner in which it was done; an exercise in betrayal and abandonment. Imagine going out for the afternoon and returning to your hotel to find that your friends had left you without a trace or explanation.

On the other hand, even more brutal was that Anita, living with Keith, became a constant reminder of this rejection—and what Brian assumed was his inadequacy. It's one thing to lose your woman but quite another to lose her to a member of your band. There's no way to forget when what your're trying to forget is always there to remind you.

And what of Keith's part in this? Perhaps, from the current perspective it seems inconceivable that Keith was the main instigator of this situation, although he certainly seemed responsible for his part. (Anita appeared to be the stronger personality at this point.) But it is indeed ironic to read Anita's comment about Brian in David Dalton's *The Rolling Stones: The First Twenty Years:* "I think literally Mick and Keith thought it out and decided to do him in because they resented him."

Appearing in court for his second drug conviction. September, 1968.

VII

Brian soon returned to London, and despite his anger and hurt, worked on composing the music for Anita's film, *A Degree of Murder.* Brian watched the film, and wrote music appropriate to its visual moods. He asked Glyn Johns to engineer it for him, which was not surprising, although the two men had never gotten along personally, they respected each other's musical talents. Glyn helped Brian select Jimmy Page for the lead guitar and Nicky Hopkins for the piano. Brian played all the other instruments: sitar, organ, dulcimer, clarinet, and harmonica. Considering Brian's depression, "the amazing thing was that the score got recorded at all," Glyn said. "Frankly, I doubted that Brian was capable of doing anything at all, including going to the loo by himself . . . . I saw him as rather a lonely character and I actually felt sorry for him. Brian worked very hard in his Courtfield flat on two little tape machines. He had all types of ideas which worked. He did it very well, and it came out amazingly. And we had a good time doing it. Brian was extremely together and confident while he was working on it. When it was finished he was both pleased and relieved. The rock 'n' roll bit which was written to fit the early murder scene was really good." Keith said of the score, "For a project nobody ever tried before—to write a whole piece of music for a film—it was good."

At the same time, in the studio, Brian sporadically contributed exotic and diverse sounds to the music. He played harpsichord on three songs: "Sittin' On a Fence," "Ride on

147

Baby," and "Take It Or Leave It." On "Please Don't Go" Brian's Bo Diddley roots resurfaced with his use of the vibrato guitar. He highlighted "Mother's Little Helper" with a 12-string guitar and "Out of Time" with marimbas.

On May 10, 1967 Brian's troubles multiplied when he was busted at Courtfield with Prince Stanislas (Stash) Klossowski de Rola. Scotland Yard's officers entered his apartment at four o'clock in the afternoon. Before they began the search, they asked Brian if he had anything other than prescription drugs in the apartment. Brian said that he only had drugs for his asthma. Looking under the covers on a bed in the living room, they found a wallet. Brian said that although the bed was his, he had never seen the wallet before, nor had Stash. In the bathroom they found a phial containing a small amount of cocaine. Under questioning, Brian's alleged reply was, "No, man, I'm not a junkie. That's not mine at all . . . that's not my scene . . . we do smoke [hash] but not cocaine, man. That's not my scene."

The two were accused of possessing cannabis resin (hashish). Scotland Yard's drug squad removed twenty-nine items from Brian's apartment for analysis. But why did the authorities call in Scotland Yard for an ordinary and quite minor drug bust? The Yard's participation pointed up the authorities' attitude toward Brian: he was to be made an example. He was to be sacrificed as retribution for all the scorn and contempt for society symbolized by the Rolling Stones.

Brian and Stash appeared at court the next day and were each given bail for 250 pounds. The proceedings lasted ten minutes. Then the five-month wait for the trial began. Brian immediately sent his parents the following telegram:

Please don't worry. Don't jump to nasty
conclusions and don't judge me too
harshly.

All my love,
Brian

To relax and to take his mind off his impending court
case, Brian traveled to America. In California, he attended
the Monterey Pop Festival dressed in full regalia. Even
though he didn't perform, he attracted a lot of attention.
Brian adorned himself in layer upon layer of exotic trea-
sures: silk ikat robes from Afghanistan, a long velvet cloak
with a sweeping collar and cuffs of white fur, an antique
lace shirt, Berber charm necklaces, enameled Berber bracelets, and assorted mammoth pendants and crosses. But his
face was lined and tired from incessant worrying about his
approaching court case. While wandering around the
grounds, where brightly dressed hippies were dancing and
singing, Brian bumped into Ralph Gleason, music journalist. Brian told Ralph how pleased he was to be at the festival, and that he found the whole experience delightful.
The spirit of community, how everyone worked together
and eagerly contributed their labor, impressed him
greatly. But Brian stayed stoned the whole time.

After the festival, Brian flew back to England and spent
much of his time with Suki Potier, a model. (Their relationship lasted about a year and a half.) Both Suki and
Anita superficially resembled Brian: they wore their
straight blond hair chin-length with long-fringed bangs. A
friend said, "The women who attracted Brian most were
the ones who looked like him." "The main reason he was
with Suki," Keith said, was she bore a passing resemblance
to Anita." Suki was devoted to Brian. "Brian used to drain
every bit of strength I had," she said. "I was the one person
he could always rely on. I think I probably loved him more

A relieved Brian with Suki Potier after being fined, instead of jailed, for drug possession. September, 1968.

than he did me . . . he was just so messed up in his mind. He used to have terrifying dreams and wake up screaming . . . His big thing was that he was so afraid he wouldn't be liked by anyone. He was so paranoid—he just thought anyone, just anyone, must hate him. He had this incredible conviction that he wouldn't live very long. Nothing would shake him from it. He believed in reincarnation. George Harrison told him, 'Action brings reaction—what you've done in one life, you'll pay for in the next.' And Brian would say, 'God, what could I have done in my last life to have it get me like this?'

"He thought of himself as a pretty useless member of society. I don't think he particularly liked himself. If it was up to him, he wished he was back in Cheltenham. Brian felt guilty about his parents being harassed by the towns-people. But they were always asking for money and he could never let them have it. He couldn't bear to give his parents money—he still couldn't forgive them for being against him and then suddenly coming on again when he started getting famous."

Shortly after his return to London, Brian suffered a breakdown. His disappointment with the group was overwhelming and incapacitating. "The other Stones accused him of being erratic towards the end," Peter Jones said. "They accused him of being unpunctual, they accused him of being unwilling to rehearse at the proper times. . . .

Brian in 1968.

You have to look then to see who's responsible for that deterioration. A lot of it could be the general ravages of having been a pop star for a long time. A lot of it could be the pressures brought from the people that (originally) you trusted and worked with towards a goal. And a lot of it could simply be the frustration you felt because the musical side was going a way that you didn't want it to." By 1967, Mick and Keith were writing *all* the music for the Stones. Song writing was a closed shop. No more old blues favorites.

Brian's psychiatrist, Dr. Leonard Henry, felt he needed residential treatment. He phoned another psychiatrist, Dr. Green (not his real name), to have Brian admitted to the Priory Nursing Home in Roehampton. Brian arrived at Priory accompanied by Suki, his chauffeur, and an entourage of friends. He refused to stay in the Home unless he could have a double room with Suki, preferably with a double bed. In a later interview, Dr. Green said, "Now one tries to be accepting and all the nice things a shrink ought to be and finally one says, 'It's absolutely not on. I will do my best to find a room for the girl elsewhere. If you like she can come and be in your room, but to put it crudely, fornication is not on unless I prescribe it. I've got to be convinced this is good for you. . . . Anyway, I'm going to put you to sleep for two days.' And I tell Suki, 'You wouldn't be any good to him and he wouldn't be any good to you anyway.'

"I feel that this insistence on having the girl there with him wasn't entirely because he wanted a friend to be close to, holding his hand because he was frightened or terrified. . . . He needed to exhibit his sexual prowess in a state of desperation—even coming to a nursing home, even saying, 'I need treatment. I'm ill. I can't live any longer if life goes on like this.' I don't mean to say he wanted to screw the girl in the nursing home. But he wanted to say, 'I can do it even there.' He wanted to psych out the guy who says, 'I screwed some lady twenty times last night.' All the men in the bar know there has never been a guy like that. But he's got to be bigger. One then suspects he can't do it at all.

" . . . I think he [Brian] suddenly wanted to treat me as one of his fans or his followers or his girlfriend or his chauffeur, as if you could really buy a doctor. . . .There was no understanding Brian about this. . . . you can still be a success, play your tin whistle, whatever, but if a guy works for you, you've got to treat him as a human being. You *cannot* ring him up at 3 A.M. three, six, nine mornings and say, 'I've decided I must go to so and so, get up and come along.' All the money in the world doesn't pay for this. But he couldn't underestand why, couldn't see it."

Brian could behave outrageously, with no thought to the gross inappropriateness of his actions. For example, the following two situations:

A platonic woman friend of Brian's told me, "We were going to stay at the Hilton Hotel in London for a night. We got up to the floor where our room was and there were shoes to be cleaned that people had put out in front of their doors. Brian ran up and down the hall swapping the shoes and throwing them down the chute. Then he ordered five portions of chips [french fries] from room service. When they arrived he tried to stuff some into the mouth of the waiter and threw the rest out the window. We weren't in there two hours before they kicked us out. They phoned up and said, 'You'll have to leave.' The house manager came up with two detectives. Brian was drunk, as usual, swearing at them and saying he refused to leave. Then they said that they would have to physically remove him. Finally, we left by the service elevator, but we were laughing so hard because we had left the bath water running."

Another time Brian pulled up at a record shop, "One Stop Records", in London's Kings Road. He emerged from his Rolls, his hair sopping wet, looking particularly bedraggled. He zoomed into the record store and asked them for a hair dryer, saying, "Dammit, I want to dry my hair. Get me something." He acted as though it didn't occur to him that it was a strange request in a record shop and that they might not have had one. He would think that they should go out and get one. Finally someone produced a blowheater which Brian used to dry his hair. He took three records, pulled them out of their jackets, and stood them up on the counter using them as a mirror while he groomed himself very carefully for about fifteen minutes.

"At times Brian felt that things were wrong, that he needed treatment and someone could offer this to him," Dr. Green continued, "but he didn't want to have this treatment except in the way *he* wanted it. Then we would get back to a reasonable rapport again. We'd talk about drugs and respectabilities and whether or not marijuana did, in fact, relax him and suit him better than Librium or Thorazine or whatever. I think he simply could not afford to do this. There was always, time and again, this stupidness or lack of judgment. . . .

"Brian became fretful that he was missing things and wanted to go out and do a recording session. We had agreed that I was unhappy about this but I said, 'Okay, you go but be back by eleven or midnight.'

"Brian came back at seven the next morning having taken something—so much of it that he couldn't really stand straight. [Without permission he] filled himself with Mandrax, which is a barbiturate sleeping tablet, and so I put him to bed and started all over again. I discovered that one of the reasons he had done this was that the chauffeur, who was not the best of men in these sorts of situations, had heard a rumor that while Jones was in the nursing home, the police planned to plant more stuff in the flat and find it. This threw him completely and he accepted that this must be the truth. Two of the three psychiatrists who saw him felt there was an incredible degree of paranoia about him. And one wasn't sure whether this was a likelihood or even a possibility or if the police were not quite as honest as I was brought up to believe.

"I don't think Brian was living in a real world. He was living in a world so totally different. . . . He resented being ordinary, or dressing like an ordinary person. He felt that he never wanted to be part of the world in which he lived and when anything interfered, his reaction was to buy it off or pretend it didn't exist. . . . He had the money and could be so different from 99.9 percent of the population. He could be what he wanted to be so long as he didn't step outside of what is a sort of funny corridor, a milky way upon which Brian Jones is walking. I only got him on the outside of these other things—which he didn't want to know about—and these things came back in anyway. I think he was hoping to grow up within them, and when he had grown up and had identified, then he could step out and be a real big person. He wanted very much to be a big important famous person in some way, not in the pop way.

". . .This is why I was trying to encourage him to get out and record his Arab music—because he had to have something for himself, all his own. He had very little. He didn't even have girlfriends that were all his own. He never really had a flat which was all his own. His musical instruments—all right, yes, they were his own. The ones he became interested in as his own were the weird and wonderful ones, like the Kentucky funny little violin thing with three strings."

In the beginning when Mick and Keith wrote their first song, the band recorded it and it was a hit, Brian didn't immediately think, "Oh, my God, I've blown it." That tune was only one song. Who would have known that they were going to continue in that direction? No one noticed Brian in tears one day because he thought he was being left out. "I doubt whether Mick and Keith ever got together and said, 'We'll leave Brian out of things,' " Peter Jones said, "but they just wouldn't ask him the kind of questions he'd been used to being asked. When you'd been together as long as they had been, you just omit certain things."

Glyn Johns said, "If I think about the first time I ever worked with Brian, when he was supposedly the leader of the band, and if I think to four or five years later, it's an amazing change. Brian still tried to keep his own identity. I don't think any of them *really* liked the fact that Mick and Keith had got the stranglehold that they did. Keith never wanted a stranglehold on the Rolling Stones. But as it turned out, because Mick and Keith wrote the material, and because *they* took an everyday interest in the running of the band and what it should and should not do, they ended up with it. In other words, the others just sat there and let it happen. Keith portrays himself as not really caring about the power in the band but I would refute that. Let's say he may care less than Mick. Mick's the really active one. But if Mick's in the process of making a decision and Keith disagrees with it, then you'll see how much Keith bloody cares. If he didn't care he would just show up when he was told."

Losing his grip on the Rolling Stones tormented Brian. He never took action about that issue until a few weeks before his death. Brian still did not want to leave the Rolling Stones because he couldn't bear the thought of being an ex-Rolling Stone. To him that would have signified failure. "But somehow along the line Brian wouldn't hack it anymore," Al Aronowitz said, "His ego had been too badly damaged by his loss of power. . . . Brian's self-esteem deteriorated right along the line until they found him in the pool."

Brian felt frustrated by not reaching his musical potential and dissatisfied by the impurity of the Stones' rhythm 'n' blues. "Brian was upset," Alexis Korner said, "by the fact that the band was not playing the same amount of proper Negro rhythm 'n' blues material as they had been when they started. He wanted to go back to playing Elmore James things and Muddy Waters things. In a way, Brian felt cheated by the switch to popularity in terms of the music. Not in terms of the feeling of being popular because he loved being popular. But he wanted both."

Though he wanted it, he couldn't have it both ways. He certainly didn't want to be playing Jagger-Richard material; that was the worst alternative. Yet he knew he was blocked, unable to create anything better. He was *stuck* being a Rolling Stone and in the band *he* created! How crazy that must have seemed to him. Caught up in his ambition to be star, to be famous, and admired, unable to give up this addiction, he had to stay in a band whose music no longer interested him. At the root he knew he couldn't depend on himself to make the ultimate sacrifices and take the risks inherent in leaving the Rolling Stones. No one suggested that Brian leave. Everyone knew that his eclectic musical contributions were a large factor in putting the Rolling Stones ahead of every other pop group.

The late rock critic Ralph Gleason said: "[Brian] was an important and fine musician with a very experimental and inquisitive mind which led him into all kinds of music . . . led him into John Coltrane and Asian music. He was obviously a major influence on the Rolling Stones, and because of that, a major influence in pop music. He was an excellent guitar player but his strength lay in the fact he was also an excellent musician capable of moving past just the playing of one instrument."

In the early fall of 1967, Brian and Suki traveled to Tangier and stayed at the Minzah Hotel. Christopher Gibbs was staying in a nearby room. "Brian had been in Tangier for quite a while with Suki," Christopher said, "and I'd been seeing him a bit. I'd not seen Suki too much because she always irritated me. Anyway, I came into my room one day around 7 P.M., feeling more dead than alive, and lay down on my bed. The telephone rang. It was Brian: 'Suki's taken an overdose. You've got to come and cope with it!' I went across and there was Suki passed out. She'd smashed up the room, broken all the mirrors, written notes, made a terrible mess, and passed out. So I got hold of the manager, I got hold of the doctor, I got hold of the ambulance and Brian said, 'Will you go to the hospital with her because I'd like to stay here?' And I said, 'No, sweetheart, this is where I get out. I've done all the rest of it. Get your ass in that ambulance immediately! Get yourself together.' Brian looked sort of faintly bemused and said, 'All right. Should we have supper later?' "

With Suki in July, 1967.

Suki was soon released from the hospital and the couple continued their vacation for another week. They returned to London, where Brian was awaiting his trial. He frequented the club scene for diversion. He spent many nights at Ronny Scotts, a jazz club. Jon Hendricks, of Lambert-Hendricks-Ross, had just arrived from America and was playing there. Hendricks was a senior citizen and guru to most of the English rock stars; Brian, Keith, Donovan, and Paul McCartney (among others) came down to see him. Six months after his arrival in England, in fact, Hendricks was voted number one jazz singer in the world by *Melody Maker*'s poll. "Brian came down to see me quite a bit at Ronny Scotts," Jon Hendricks said. "I was there six nights a week and Brian was there almost all the time. Brian was a big jazz fan and would go to see everybody. He was very quiet, never made his presence known. Once I was standing and talking with a crowd of people around me and Brian was there. If somebody hadn't pointed out that it was Brian, I never would have known."

This quiet side of Brian was also shown to complete strangers. A salesman at a Carnaby Street boutique that outfitted Brian said, "Brian was very, very inward, very deep. He never said much. He was always polite. Not the politeness of a proper gentleman who would get up when you left the room, but the politeness brought about by sincerity. He just didn't seem to be in the right business."

One night at a club called The Speakeasy, Brian was having drinks with Suki and a few friends when he noticed an attractive blond (with hair like his) at the bar. "Brian and his friends descended upon me," Debby Scott said. "Suki started to flip out immediately. Brian started picking at this furry little jacket that I had on. His attitude was, 'Oh yes, who are you? Somebody please introduce us.' I thought he looked like a little court jester or clown. He was small with short little legs. He was wearing something with puffy sleeves and tight red velvet trousers. If he had bells on his toes it would have been perfect. Brian asked me to come over to his house for a party. At first I said 'No,' but he kept asking me to go back and have a few drinks and said, 'Don't worry, my driver will take you home.' So I did eventually end up going back there. Suki was actually very upset and stormed off into the night, but Brian didn't seem to particularly care. One of his friends kept saying, 'Now, Brian, you've got to do what *you* want to do. You have to do what *you* want to do.' Brian later asked me if I came back to his flat because I liked him or because he was a Rolling Stone. I told him it was because he was a Rolling Stone. After I said that his eyes got very big. He was obviously shocked that I had been so honest with him. And since he was tripping on acid his expressions were very open. He couldn't act cool. Brian talked about his court case. I said, 'How dare they take four years out of your life for smoking a joint,' and he kept saying, 'YEAH, YEAH, four years out of my life.' "

Debby worked as a waitress at Blases and Brian began visiting her a few afternoons a week. Blases' manager, Jim Carter-Fae, invariably let Debby leave with Brian no matter what time Brian came. One afternoon, when they were out in the country, Brian filled the back seat of the car with dead leaves from the side of the road—because they looked so beautiful and sounded nice when you sat on them.

Brian and Debby saw each other sporadically over the next year, usually when Suki was out of town. They took a lot of acid together. Although Brian never had a bad acid trip with Debby, he did have them with other people. "It is perfectly reasonable to learn to live with yourself by building certain barriers against those parts of yourself which you are unable to control," Alexis Korner said. "It is very possible that when Brian took acid he was faced with certain parts of himself that he just did not wish to see, didn't wish to know about, and could not cope with."

Meanwhile, Brian sometimes busied himself by working on the Stones' *Their Satanic Majesties Request* album. Although he contributed the smallest amount he ever had for an album, the quality of his work remained intact. In Glyn Johns' opinion Brian personally saved the track "2000 Light Years From Home" from disaster, by changing the song's direction with the mellotron. Another one of the Stones' engineers said, "Brian was excellent at the mellotron. He really was brilliant. I haven't heard anybody get out of a mellotron either the rhythm or the rest of the structure that Brian got."

Brian returned to court on October 30, 1967, and pleaded guilty to smoking cannabis and allowing his apartment to be used for smoking. The judge sentenced him to nine months in Wormwood Scrubs (a jail) and Brian began serving his term that night. Eight Rolling Stones fans, among them Mick Jagger's brother and Suzy Creamcheese, a personality made famous by the Mothers of Invention, protested Brian's sentence in front of the courthouse. The eight were arrested and remanded up to four weeks for abusive behavior and damaging a police van.

Keith, who spent a night in Wormwood Scrubs (he, too, had been sentenced for one year for allowing people to smoke in his house), described it to a *Rolling Stone* writer: "Wormwood Scrubs is 150 years old, man. I wouldn't even want to play there, much less live there. They take me inside. They don't give you a knife and fork, they give you a spoon with very blunt edges so you can't do yourself in. They don't give you a belt, in case you hang yourself. It's that bad in there . . . then, you're given your cell. And they start knockin' on the bars at six in the morning to wake you up. . . . The first thing you do automatically when you wake up is drag the chair to the window. It's an automatic reaction. That one little square of sky, tryin' to reach it.

". . .Then there's the hour walk when you have to keep moving, round in a courtyard. Cats comin' up behind me, it's amazing, they can talk without moving their mouths. 'Want some hash? Want some acid?' Take acid? In there?

"Most of the prisoners were really great. 'What you doin' in here?' Bastards. They just wanted to get you. They filled me in. 'They been waiting for you in here for ages,' they said . . . .They took all the new prisoners to have their photographs taken sitting on a swivel stool—looked like an execution chamber. Really hard. Face and profile. Those are the sort of things they'll do automatically if they pick you up in America; you get fingerdabs and photographs. In England, it's a much heavier scene. You don't get photographed and fingerprinted until you've been convicted."

"Then they take you to the padre and the chapel and the library; you're allowed one book and they show you where you're going to work and that's it."

When Dr. Green heard that Brian had been sentenced to nine months in jail, he was worried that the first thing they'd do would be to cut Brian's hair. Dr. Green phoned the prison medical officer and interceded on Brian's behalf. Brian spent a miserable night in jail with prison officers saying, "We finally got one of those bloody longhairs."

That evening, Dr. Green, at the request of Brian's lawyers, went to see the judge in his chambers at the Royal Halls of Justice. Green cleared the case for Brian on the grounds that he thought Brian was ill. Still, he felt the chances of Brian winning his appeal were small: "A hell of a lot was stacked against him—public feeling, judicial feeling. . . . It seemed obvious that the Establishment had said, 'Get a few people who are popular with the adolescents and let's nail them.' This to me was the tenor of the time." Although Brian originally had been denied bail, he was then released on 750 pounds. Upon leaving, Brian said,

"All I want is to be left alone." He had found his evening in jail agonizing. The idea of living in jail for the next nine months seemed unbearable as he sat in his cell waiting for the minutes to crawl by.

A few days later, the Stones' publicist issued a statement: "The Stones will go on, there's no doubt about that." In other words, the Stones were telling the world that if Brian were incarcerated they would definitely continue without him.

The court of appeal took a most unusual step of consulting an independent psychiatrist, Walter Neustatter. Neustatter was described by Green as "having done more forensic psychiatry than any other ten psychiatrists put together." Green and Neustatter unexpectedly ran into each other a few days before the appeal trial. At that time, Neustatter told Green that Brian seemed like quite a nice boy to him. Although he was put off by the bear skin "rug" (it was a coat) that Brian wore and those sorts of things, he thought Brian was a very sensitive person with considerable talent. He also thought Brian was having enormous difficulties finding himself as a person. Unlike his usual procedure of seeing a man only once before his trial, Neustatter saw Brian four times during the period of June through October of 1967. He prepared the following report for Brian's appeal:

> "His I.Q. 133. Intellectual functioning shows assets in his range of general knowledge, abstract reasoning capacity, social awareness and vocabulary. He does not reveal signs of formal thought disorder or psychotic disturbance of thought processes. However, Mr. Jones' thought processes do reveal some weakening of his reality ties as a result of intense free-floating anxiety. He currently tends to

feel very threatened by the world about him as a result of his increasingly inadequate control of aggressive instinctual impulses. This repressive control seems to be breaking down and he often resorts to conspicuous denial of the threat created by the breakthrough of these impulses into consciousness. At times he projects these aggressive feelings so that he feels a victim of his environment; at others he introjects them, resulting in significant depressive tendencies and associated suicidal risk. Mr. Jones' sexual problems are closely interrelated to his difficulties of aggression—that is, he experiences very intense anxiety surrounding phallic and sadistic sexuality because of the implicit aggressive strivings. However, these phallic strivings are also in conflict with his gross passive dependency needs. This conflict prevents any mature heterosexual adjustment—indeed, he withdraws from any genuine heterosexual involvement. These sexual difficulties reinforce Mr. Jones' considerable emotional immaturity and effect gross confusion and identification. He vacillates between a passive, dependent child with a confused image of an adult on the one hand, and an idol of pop culture on the other. He is still very involved with Oedipal fixations. He is very confused about the maternal and paternal role in these. Part of his confusion would seem to be the very strong resentment he experiences toward his dominant and controlling mother who rejected him and blatantly favored his sister. In conclusion, it is my considered opinion that Mr. Jones is, at present, in an extremely precarious state of emotional adjustment as a result of his unresolved problems with aggressive impulses and sexual identification. His grasp on reality is fragile because of the debilitating effect of intense anxiety and conflicts surrounding these problems. Much of his anxiety is currently localized onto his potential imprisonment but its underlying sources are more deeply rooted. He thus urgently needs psychotherapy to assist in mustering his considerable personality resources and capacity for insight to contain his anxiety. Otherwise, his prognosis is very poor. Indeed, it is very likely that his imprisonment could precipitate a complete break with reality, a psychotic breakdown and significantly increase the suicidal risk for this man."

About five weeks later, December 12, Brian's appeal was heard. The evening papers featured two-inch headlines that read "THE MIND OF BRIAN JONES." Three psychiatrists predicted disaster if Brian served his prison sentence. Based on their testimony, the court fined Brian 1,000 pounds and put him on probation for three years, on condition that Brian continue to see Dr. Green. Brian later resented having to meet with his parole officer every two weeks and having to ask permission when he wanted to leave the country. He especially resented that his parole officer was an older man who talked a great deal about his own children. Brian wanted the parole officer to talk about Brian. Dr. Green told the court that upon admittance to the Priory Nursing Home, Brian was "anxious, considerably depressed, and potentially suicidal. I found it, at first, difficult to get at the young man under the panoply of the pop singer." When Brian left the home, his condition had improved and since that time Dr. Green had seen Brian about once a week.

"I found a pleasant young man," Dr. Green told the court, "of very high intelligence who had a sensible and, it seemed to me, realistic plan for the future. But he was easily depressed and thwarted. What seemed to him overwhelming problems made him anxious and depressed. He has a history of depressive mental illness. My concern since his last appearance in court has been to calm his apprehensions as well as treat his underlying illness. He has been an extremely frightened young man. I think that if one put a reefer within a half a mile of Brian Jones he would start running."

"The periods while he was waiting to be tried, and then for the appeal hearing, had an astounding effect on Brian," Dr. Green continued, "and prison would be disastrous." He added that Brian would like to go to a university and "was certainly capable of it. He has not a great deal of confidence in himself. He is not sure of his identity and I think to put him in prison would finish him as a person. He would not recover. It would be a tremendous blow to his 'growing up.' "

A second psychiatrist, Dr. Henry, who had seen Brian eight times that year, told the court that Brian "was a very sick man." He considered Brian "a very emotional and unstable person who, in circumstances not intolerable to a less neurotic personality, might well make an attempt on his life. Prison would arouse such guilt feelings that any attempt to enable him to come to terms with his emotional problems would probably be impossible."

The third psychiatrist, Dr. Walter Neustatter, told of his four sessions with Brian: "He came in most extraordinary clothes which one could only describe as flamboyant.

I think he had gold trousers and something which looked like a fur rug. When I asked Brian about his outfit he said that uniformity in males rather frightened him. But surprisingly I found the man inside the clothes quiet and thoughtful, with a courteous manner."

One of the most persuasive points in Brian's defense was made by his attorney, Mr. James Comyn, who said that Brian would like the young to know that drugs were bad; nobody should take an example from what he had done or seek to follow him. His fans should remember that drugs solved no problems for him, but created them.

Mr. Comyn went on to say: "Brian has, perhaps the worse for him, been catapulted to fame and that has imposed an additional strain on an already fragile mental makeup. The period of time since the offenses has meant more suffering for him than perhaps it would for 99 out of 100 people. It may sound trite but he has suffered every single day since then, a suffering that cannot be removed and may be regarded as penalty enough for the offenses he has committed."

Comyn said that because Brian Jones was in the public eye, it warranted the court making an example of him. Maybe the judge made the punishment fit the man when the right approach should be to make the punishment fit the crime. Brian had given parties at his home and perhaps through "weakmindedness" had not been able to prevent people at the party from smoking cannabis. "None of the people at the parties was before the court," continued Comyn. "Jones is carrying the burden of everybody."

When the court decided not to send Brian to prison, Lord Parker, the Lord Chief Justice, told Brian, "Remember, this is a degree of mercy which the court has shown. It is not a let-off. You cannot go boasting, saying you have been let-off. You are still under the control of the court. If you fail to cooperate with the probation officer or the doctor or you commit another offense of any sort, you will be brought back and punished afresh for this offense. And you know the sort of punishment you will get."

Brian left the courtroom silent. His only statement was "I'm very happy to have my freedom." The only Stone to attend the appeal was Mick, and Dr. Green mentioned that Brian was "pathetically pleased."

". . . He gave the Rolling Stones instruments as colorfully diverse as peacock feathers, and as proud."

VIII

1968began with the Stones hard at work on the *Beggar's Banquet* album (the name was suggested by Christopher Gibbs). Brian was with them when they met at Keith's country house, Redlands, to rehearse. A tape I heard of one of those get-togethers contained bits of conversation and early takes of "No Expectations" as well as other songs that were not included on the album: a gutsy Muddy Waters tune with Brian playing fine bottleneck guitar, Mick on the harmonica and Nicky Hopkins at the piano. For one particular song, Mick asked Brian how the harmonica should be played. Brian said that he didn't know. After the electronically psychedelic *Satanic Majesties, Beggar's Banquet* marked a return to the Stones' roots of blues harp and slide guitar. Jimmy Miller, who produced *Banquet,* said of Brian: "As a musician he should be remembered for the brilliant bottleneck country guitar work on *Beggar's Banquet;* for his interpretation of the blues played honestly, as a white man." Miller referred most likely to "No Expectations," "Jigsaw Puzzle," and "Salt of the Earth."

After the session when the Stones recorded "Jumping Jack Flash," Brian called Ronny at around 6 A.M. and told her, "We've been in the studio all morning and we're going back to rock 'n' roll. They've got this 'Jumping Jack Flash' and it's really great." Ronny commented, "Brian knew then that it was all over for him, but he was pleased for *them.*" How ironic that he referred to the Rolling Stones as *they,* not *we.*

Jimmy Miller said of this period: "In his last eighteen months with the group, Brian was plagued with personal problems, and his musical differences with the rest of the group were increasingly apparent. He was entirely a musician and never quite adapted to the commercial and image aspects of being a Stone. . . . When the sessions [*Beggar's Banquet*] first started, Brian came up to me and said he didn't think he would be able to contribute much. I didn't push him, I just asked Mick what the situation was and Mick said, 'Look, you can't force him—he'll be okay.' And he was right. When we started working he really got into it and started to get excited. Then he came up to me and apologized for having had any doubts at the beginning. . . . When he's doing something that really interests him he's almost a different character."

Yet Brian often did not show up for sessions. He would call the studio and say that he couldn't come in because he had a headache, or a stomachache, or a toothache. Brian was reportedly taking a lot of Mandrax (Methaqualone or Quaaludes, a hypnotic sedative—classified in England as a dangerous drug.) Supposedly, he alternated Mandrax with amphetamines.

Around this time, Jean-Luc Godard made the film *Sympathy for the Devil*. The movie intersperses the Stones' development of the song "Sympathy for the Devil" through its sketchy beginnings to the completed version, with Godard's commentary on political revolutionaries. Mick receives the focus of attention from the band members and the camera, while Brian appears the outsider. At one point, Brian timidly suggests that Nicky Hopkins play something on the piano, which Mick either does not hear or ignores. When the movie ends, Brian is sitting on the floor in the dark, smoking what appears to be a joint; the others are grouped together.

At another informal session with Jack Nitzsche and Ry Cooder, Brian entered in a desperate mood. Nitzsche recalled in an interview published in *Creem* magazine. "He came up to me, looking pretty shaky, and asked me where he fit in. I told him to just pick up a guitar and start playing. Then he walked up to Mick and asked, 'What should I play?' Mick told him, 'You're a member of the band, Brian, play whatever you want.' So he played something, but Mick stopped him and said, 'No, Brian, not that—that's no good.' So Brian asked him again what to play and Mick told him again to play whatever he wanted. So Brian played something else, but Mick cut him off again—'No, that's no good either, Brian.'

"Brian then tried the congas. Jagger beat out a rhythm for him to follow but he couldn't match it. Brian was just not built like Mick—he wasn't as loose, so the beat sounded stiffer. Brian ended up drunk in the corner, stamping his foot out of beat, and blowing harmonica with a bloodied mouth. Jagger stared at him icily, threw his coat over his shoulder, and exited the studio."

Brian's girlfriend at this time was Linda Keith, a model who also dated Keith Richard. (He had stopped seeing Suki for awhile.) On March 16, Brian went out to a recording session and told Linda he would be back in three hours. When he stopped in at home around 9 P.M., Linda was sleeping. He went out again to the studio and when he returned, just after twelve, he found the police at the apartment. Linda had gotten the idea that there was another woman in Brian's life and had tried to kill herself. After swallowing the pills, however, she had taken off her clothes, phoned friends to inform them of her impending death (a mysterious phone call from a woman alerted the police) and locked the front door so that the police had to smash it down. The next day the newspapers featured an article entitled, "Stone's Girl Naked in Drug Drama." This did not help Brian and his much-desired law-abiding image.

Brian's landlord immediately evicted him from the apartment. The housekeeper told the press, "Although Mr. Jones' belongings are still in there we don't want him back. The landlord gave him half an hour to clear out when he had returned home on Saturday morning to find the girl had been taken to hospital." Of the eviction Brian said, "I was absolutely shattered when the landlord of the flat asked the police to have me removed. He said, 'It's because you are trespassing. We don't want your kind in this place.'

"I explained that I rented the flat at thirty pounds a week for my chauffeur and I only lived here when I was working in town." Linda and Brian broke up shortly thereafter.

In the spring of 1968, Brian went to Marrakesh to record the G'naoua. Glyn Johns accompanied Brian and engineered the taping. The G'naoua musicians consist of about fifteen males ranging in age from a very old man (the leader) to several small children. Two musicians beat out complex rhythms on steel drums and the others play large metal castanets.

Brian was the first rock star to record ethnic music. "Brian was very much interested in other people's cultures," Ronny Money said, "and let's face it, at that particular time in the sixties, nobody was interested in anything except getting out of it, dressing up, and having a great time—I was involved in that too. But the beautiful thing about Brian was that he didn't think *he* was the only person. He knew that there were corners of the world, villages in outer Siberia where somebody was probably sitting down and playing better than him and would never be heard. In fact, he said that to me—not with the intention of exploiting them, but with the intention of learning something from them."

By recording the G'naoua, and later, the Master Musicians of Jajouka, Brian opened a new direction in popular music. In January 1975, the Sunday *New York Times* discussed this trend in an article entitled, "Trance Music—A Trend of the 1970s" by Robert Palmer:

> *Westerners have traditionally preferred music with harmonic variety, melodic appeal, developmental interest. But trance music—an admittedly imprecise term for the many diverse approaches to organized musical repetition—has been gaining acceptance here and in Europe.*
>
> *"In pop, black discotheque-oriented bands and European electronic groups . . . are beginning to explore the possibilities of rhythmic and modal repetition, which seeks through absolute control of limited musical means to induce relaxation, contemplation, euphoria, and other psychological states, rather than merely provide soundtracks for chemically induced ones.*
>
> *". . . complex drumming is found in Morocco, where trance music is usually polyrhythmic. The effects noted there— people in trances are liable to leap into the air, walk on hot coals, and sustain self-inflicted wounds which heal with remarkable rapidity—are more violent than those of shamanist ceremonies. Laboratory studies of rhythmic stimulation suggest that the accompanying*

rhythms, especially multiples of the main rhythm, heighten the average subject's response. Regular swaying, jumping, dancing and spinning, all features of Moroccan 'folk trance,' serve to reinforce the initial stimulation. The decibel level and insistence of the drumming doubtless inhibit the transmission of pain to the conscious brain.

Throughout their Moroccan trip, according to Glyn, when Brian was not directly involved in recording the G'naoua, he was "non compus mentis. When somebody gets to the state where you can't even get them to do anything or talk to them, it gets rather boring. So obviously I let Brian know I was extremely bored and he felt badly."

Although the two were barely speaking, Glyn still held Brian's musical ideas in high regard: "Brian's brilliant idea," Glyn said, "was to record as much as was possible of the G'naoua, listen to the tapes back in London and decide what was usable, and then take the tapes to America and try to get a black soul rhythm section to play along with it. The G'naoua musicians were black—as opposed to the lighter Arab and Berber people. Brian's theory was that black music in America originated in Africa—so it would be a symbolic statement, musically as well as ethnically—and quite a profound one at that."

However, after repeated playbacks, Brian decided that the tapes were not as good as he had hoped. He discovered that they had used a slightly defective recording machine which registered a hiss audible above the music. Although Brian probably could have removed the hiss, still the tapes were disappointingly incoherent.

Back in London, Brian resumed his relationship with Debby Scott during the spring of 1968. The two enjoyed each other's company, but Brian's manic-depressive behavior complicated their friendship. One afternoon in mid-May, for example, Brian phoned Debby and invited her to visit him in his room at London's Imperial Hotel. When Debby arrived she found Brian difficult to talk to, and his coldness upset her. They both felt uneasy. Finally, Brian, after grappling with Debby, awkwardly tried to push her out the door, saying, "Don't make me degrade you."

Debby said, "Look, just be honest with me. Wasn't there something there?"

"Aw, chicks . . . they're always trying to fuck me up . . . and I don't have to be honest with anyone."

Debby made a pride-saving exit when the phone rang.

A week later she received a phone call from Brian: "Whatcha' doing? Get your ass over here!" She shot over to Brian's flat and they dropped acid together. Brian told her he thought the police were watching him. He was certain they had tapped his phone and every so often he would pick up the receiver and yell at the dial tone: "IF YOU WANT TO KNOW IF I USE DRUGS—YES I DO." Brian and Debby did not say a word to each other for about two hours. Finally Debby stared searchingly at Brian's face for reassurance. When this failed, she began crying hysterically. Brian left the room and phoned a friend, imploring her to come over immediately. The friend arrived and Debby left at 6 A.M. Brian and his friend watched from the upstairs window as Debby strolled down an empty King's Road. A lone police car approached, slowed down, and continued down the street.

An hour later, alone in his flat, Brian went to the refrigerator for a piece of chicken. While he stood vacantly chewing on a drumstick the police arrived. Brian froze in terror. Whisked off to court, he pleaded guilty and was fined fifty pounds for possession of marijuana. The judge released him on 2,000 pounds bail.

Many of his friends felt this second bust would destroy Brian. "When someone said to me, 'Did you hear that Brian Jones has been busted?' I felt like I had been socked in the chest," Debby Scott said. "I knew it would finish Brian. It was like a big fist had come down from the sky that had written on it: 'We're gonna' smash you. We're gonna' crush you, Brian Jones!' Brian really thought he would go to prison—and it was a definite possiblity. No one else got it like Brian. It was at the height of hippiedom; the psychedelic age where people with long hair who took acid were menaces, threats to society. And Brian Jones, as a member of the Rolling Stones, was a number one target. They wanted to make a public spectacle of Brian Jones."

Mick Jagger, in an interview in *Crawdaddy Magazine*, published in July 1974, talked about the effects of being busted and put in jail: "Now if you do that kind of thing to some people it makes them strong and if you do it to others it can quickly destroy them, and it destroyed Brian which is very sad. He just couldn't take it . . . Brian came really close to doing six months. . . . He was followed all the time, but we all were. It was a systematic campaign of harassment [which] brought Brian down and destroyed [the musical side] of him as well."

The day after his arrest, Brian withdrew to the nursing home where he had gone before. Linda Lawrence, hearing of Brian's breakdown, took Julian for a visit. Julian wore a white silk suit which Linda had made and Brian, ironically, had on a similar white suit. Suki was sitting in the room when Linda arrived, and Brian led Linda into the hall to talk, realizing that her presence might upset Suki. Linda felt that she had made some contact with Brian—an opening, a shy warmth. Brian stared hard into Julian's face for a few minutes and then felt frightened. He later talked to Ronny about it: "Seeing Julian frightened me because he's totally untouched by any of that. He's so pure." Ronny replied, "It's almost like looking at him and seeing your lost innocence."

Debby Scott tried many times to reach Brian at the nursing home. Finally late one night Brian phoned her and said, "Did you bust me? You busted me. I know it." Debby tried to convince Brian that she had nothing to do with what had happened.

Brian had enjoyed Debby's company, but she did not have the glamourous image of a superstar's lady. Brian once told her, "I like your face. I don't know if everybody would like your face, but I do." Debby Scott, Ronny Money, even Linda Lawrence (to some extent) formed a small group of people who did not threaten Brian. They were women with whom he could talk intimately, act naturally, and not worry about his cool.

Brian had separated his public role and friends from his private life. He felt self-conscious with public people like Mick, Marianne, and Keith. Once, when Brian showed Debby a photograph of himself with Keith, he mentioned that he thought Keith looked like an angel. "Brian was very threatened by the idea of what Mick, Marianne, Keith and Anita thought of him," Debby said. "In Brian's eyes they were the big stars. Brian thought Mick and Marianne *seemed* to be okay; Keith and Anita *seemed* okay—and here he was out in the cold. They didn't do anything to particularly help Brian.

"I remember being over at Brian's place . . . apparently Marianne never liked Brian very much, and used to run him down to Mick. Anyway, Brian rang up Mick for something. When Brian got off the phone he 'said, 'You know what Mick said? "Why don't you get over here, you

FREAK?" ' But the way Brian said it to me—I could tell it was like a bolt going through him when Mick said it. Mick didn't say it to be cruel, although Mick knew that Brian was paranoid. Instead of trying to be sensitive about it, Mick would try to joke about it. In other words, let's say you know someone feels terrible about some ugly dress they have on, but they're trying not to show it. So instead of saying, 'Don't you look lovely?' you say, 'Oh, come on you horrible old slob in your horrible old dress. I dig you.' That was what Mick was trying to do."

On June 11, 1968, Brian's court date was set—for September 26. Needing an escape, he was lured once again to Tangier. In the summer of 1968, Brian visited the tiny village of Jajouka, outside of Tangier, and recorded the music of their master musicians. This effort culminated in an album, released posthumously by the Rolling Stones, entitled *Brian Jones Presents the Pipes of Pan at Jajouka*. Brian was assisted on the project by George Chkiantz, an engineer who had worked with the Stones since 1966, Suki (their on-off relationship was on again) and Brion Gysin, who was famous for having given Alice B. Toklas her brownie recipe.

It had been Brion Gysin's idea to bring Brian Jones to Jajouka. Gysin, a writer and painter, was running a restaurant aptly named "A Thousand and One Nights" in Tangier. There, he met a Moroccan painter named Hamri, and they quickly became friends. Hamri provided musicians from his native village (Jajouka) to play at the restaurant. Gysin, impressed by the quality of the music, wanted to know more about it and eventually Hamri took him up to the village where he discovered that their annual festival consisted of the relics of a pre-Roman celebration: The Rites of Pan. He thought the Jajouka should be recorded, and even tried, unsuccessfuly, to record it himself.

"Gysin was the sort of person that Jones would look out for," George Chkiantz said. "Jones had been into (William) Burroughs, who was with Gysin in Tangier. I don't think if you were Brian Jones you could have avoided tripping over Gysin."

When Brian had the recording of the Festival, he immediately sent for George, who was in London. George arrived in Tangier at 8 A.M. An energetic Brian and Suki greeted him at the airport. (George was so shocked that he sent a telegram back to the Rolling Stones' office saying that Brian was even awake at 8 A.M.) "Brian was glad to see me, was beaming and looking very good," George said. "He was not spaced out. Brian was very excited and a perfect host. To get me feeling comfortable, he tried to explain what he knew of Morocco."

George, Suki, and Brian picked up Gysin and Hamri. Gysin explained that Suki would present a problem because women and men were strictly segregated in the village, and she would have to stay with the Berber women. Suki insisted on accompanying them, and Brian wanted her there. She eventually cut her hair very short and dressed in pants to look as much like a man as possible.

The five started out for Jajouka. The acoustics of the place are amazing. Although the village is far from the ocean, you can hear the waves crashing against the rocks in the distance. The villagers moved their dogs a quarter of a mile away for the festival, yet on the second side of Brian's album a dog is heard barking through the stillness of the night.

"After a brief rest, we started recording," George said. "They set up a synopsis, musically, of the festival with some kids dancing as well." Brian was fascinated; here he was recording genuine folklore. "We got the recording gear going by about sundown and continued until 4 A.M. The villagers thought we were very funny. They had only seen about ten or fifteen white men or non-native villagers. Very few of the villagers actually came out of the compound or went very far. They were very much virgins to the rest of the world. I really got the impression that if we were green and had antlers we would have been no more funny. The younger people put the tapes on and listened to them, but the elders decided it was magic that they wouldn't get involved in.

"That night we stayed in the village after finally getting to bed around 5 A.M. They evacuated a room and found some beds for us.We all crashed out together. Brian and Suki were sleeping in one end of the room and I was in the other, with Gysin on the front porch. They let us sleep until eleven in the morning, which was already outrageously late by their standards. Then at eleven, they got together every flute and reed player in the village. I suddenly heard this slight shuffling around the door and all of a sudden heard this massive discord which they blew for about five seconds—a huge amount of noise. After which there was a series of twitters and people disappeared into the distance. By the time we put on some kind of clothes and looked out, there was no one in sight. That was our alarm call.

"We began recording again. There was one really fantastic thing on the second side during the lengthy flute solo. It really isn't a solo—the two flute players are changing over parts—one man plays the continual note, the held note, and the other man plays against it. After so many bars or so much time (like about thirty seconds) they swap over. You can hear them do this because one of the men had a cold and you can hear him sniffling. That sniffling is the speed at which he is breathing, while he's holding the note. They use the same technique as Roland Kirk, who manages to play instruments forever and ever—without any breath pauses. They hold a pouch of air in their mouths by controlling their cheeks, keeping a continual blowing motion down while they are breathing in. Then they send the air from their lungs into the pouch."

The group spent the day at Jajouka. Brian smoked kif and brought along some morphine and asthma medication, neither of which he used. Brion Gysin (in a 1971 *Rolling Stone*) related the following prophetic anecdote about that day: " . . .The musicians were working just four or five feet away, ahead of us in the courtyard where the animals usually are. It was getting to be time to eat, and suddenly two of the musicians came along with a snow white goat. The goat disappeared off into the shadows with the two musicians, one of whom was holding a long knife which Brian suddently caught the glitter of, and he started to get up, making a sort of funny noise, and he said, 'That's me! And everybody picked up on it right at once and said, 'Yeah, right, it looks just like you.' It was perfectly true, he had this fringe of blond hair hanging right in front of his eyes, and we said, 'Of course that's you!' Then about twenty minutes later we were eating this goat's liver on shish kebab sticks."

Brion Gysin described the rites and music of Jajouka in the liner notes for Brian's album:

> Magic calls itself The Other Method for controlling matter and knowing space. In Morocco, magic is practiced more assiduously than hygiene though, indeed, ecstatic dancing to music of the brotherhoods may be called a form of psychic hygiene. You know your own music when you hear it one day. You fall into line and dance until you pay the piper. . . .

Pan, Bou Jeloud, the Father of Skins, dances through either moonlight nights in his hill village, Jajouka, to the wailing of his hundred Master Musicians. Down in the towns, far away by the seaside, you can hear the wild whimper of his oboe-like *raitas*; a faint breath of panic borne on the wind. Below the rough palisade of giant blue cactus surrounding the village on its hilltop, the music flows in streams to nourish and fructify the terraced fields below.

Inside the village the thatched houses crouch low in their gardens to hide the deep cactus-lined lanes. You come through their maze to the broad village green where the pipers are piping; fifty *raitas* banked against a crumbling wall below sheet lightning to shatter the air. Fifty wild flutes blow up a storm in front of them, while a platoon of small boys in long belted robes and brown wool turbans drums like young thunder. All the villagers dressed in best white, swirl in great circles and coil around one wildman in skins.

Brian included these comments in the liner notes:

. . . Jajouka has yet to have a road built thereto; is without electricity, plumbing; in short all the "comforts" without which a majority of us would cry out in agonized discomfort. In fact, there is no school as such. All knowledge and culture is passed down from mother to child until the age of twelve, at which age the father-community watches over the tender years of the boys, and young girls are not further to be seen until married off.

What exists here is a specifically chosen representation of the type of music which is played and chanted during the festival. The pieces and therefore the climaxes are necessarily shortened and when one considers that many of these chants continue for hours and hours, one will realize this necessity. We apologize for the virtual inaudibility of the lead singer during the chanting of the women but she and the others are singing not to an audience of mortals, but rather they are chanting an incantation to those of another plane, and while we were recording her, she hid her beautiful voice behind the drum she was playing. It was not for our ears. Anyway, we hope we have captured the spirit and magic of Jajouka.

Back in Tangier after the festival, Brian resumed his normal self-destructive habits. One evening, George related, "We got back to the hotel around 5 A.M. Brian stood on the balcony of our suite yelling, *Salaam Alekhem*, (which means 'peace' and 'greetings') to every passerby. Anyone who said *Salaam Alekhem* back, Brian would say 'Hi' to. Anyone who didn't, received a torrent of abuse, beginning with 'Cunt.' Then all of a sudden, Brian turned around and said, 'What's "good morning" in Arabic?'

"I said, 'You've been saying it all morning. It's *Salaam Alekhem.*'

"Brian said, 'No. Phone room service. I'm sure that I've got it wrong.'

"I thought it was early to phone room service just to say some idiotic thing. Brian was so insistent I was unable to do anything about it. He kept saying, 'It's all right. Just phone them. I must know.'

"And as I turned around, Brian fell over—he suddenly was completely paralyzed and fell over like a statue. Fortunately, he didn't go over the porch. He just hit his head. I was quite alarmed, but Suki said, 'Brian does this every night. Just throw a blanket over him and leave him there.'"

Seeing Brian function so well in Jajouka surprised George. Prior to the trip, he had considered Brian's presence at the sessions as something of a joke. "Brian would normally get some minor part given to him and was promised an overdub which he either did or didn't get," George said. "Mick and Keith would relegate these positions. Those two work very much in collusion; always have and always will. I did think it was a bit much the way they were going on about him. But then on the one hand, at the time I was madder about it than now—because I have a lot of experience in these kinds of things. Somebody like Brian was no longer capable of fulfilling a real function in the group. Of couse, *he* still thought he was. I'm sure Mick and Keith did what they considered their best in trying to reach him, but it obviously wasn't good enough. The saddest thing in the whole world was to watch Brian spend three and a half hours trying to put a reed in a saxophone and failing because he was too drunk to make it. Watching this for three and a half hours gets beyond a joke, but nobody could stop him. Everybody tried. He was absolutely determined to get it done. We had to wait until he got thirsty and give him another Mandrax, and send him to sleep.

"I don't think he ever achieved anything like his potential anyway. He was a brilliant player in his own way, but he was getting more and more freaked out. What he did in the end, musically, was very good once he got going. Brian would go along and suddenly get some idea and you'd wonder whether he was completely crazy or not . . . like he'd put a harp on some song. But he was a multi-instrumentalist; he could pick up any instrument and by dint of bashing away at it for long enough he could get what he wanted. I think he was bored by the guitar.

"Brian, although a very creative person, was not equal to withstanding all the pressures and his mind was gradually going. I would say that nobody was of much help to him. He didn't have the right kind of friends. His friends tended to be an awful lot of yes-men who were mainly after the money. After we returned from Morocco, Brian was still open to me, but it was difficult to contact him—to make any *real* contact. It was like talking to a shadow. He just wasn't there inside of his body. We worked on the Jajouka tapes together. First we sifted through the material because we had about ten hours' worth. Brian wanted to produce Moroccan music which the Stones could overdub."

In February of 1969, the people of Jajouka celebrated their annual festival. They honored Brian by inviting him to be Bou Jaloud. Bou Jaloud has the privilege of wearing a goat skin, which has been freshly stripped off of a live goat, for seven days and nights. Brian felt both flattered and frightened, and was relieved to decline because the Stones had booked sessions through February. When the sessions began, Brian remarked to George, "Do you know where we should be right now? We should be recording the real festival. They are very offended because I haven't come. It's the kind of invitation you don't refuse."

In the early part of 1975, another album was released which records the Master Musicians of Jajouka. Stephen Davis reviewed it in *Rolling Stone:* "The Jajouka Masters are very grateful to Brian Jones, and the schoolhouse where they train their sons is the center of the world Brian Jones cult. On the wall is David Bailey's famous portrait of Brian, and they have a song . . . called 'Brahim Jones,' with words to the effect that the yellow-haired man who helped give their music to the world is with them now and forever to come. It's a frenetic Moroccan jump song with a few English words, and the portrait of Brian seems to leap in its frame whenever they sing it:

Ah Brahim Jones
Jajouka Rolling Stone
Ah Brahim Jones
Jajouka really stoned

The Stones toured Europe during 1967. In 1968, they performed at the *New Musical Express'* Pollwinners Concert, playing "Jumping Jack Flash," their newest single, and "Satisfaction" before they accepted their award. Their only other major performance in 1968 was *The Rock 'n' Roll Circus*, taped in December. Originally done as a BBC-TV special, it has never been shown commercially in the United States. The Circus included the Stones, Marianne Faithfull, John Lennon, Yoko Ono, Peter Townshend, Roger Daltrey, Danyale Luna, and Eric Clapton. Aside from the rock stars, there were plate-spinners, a boxing kangaroo, acrobats, clowns, midgets, and tigers. Jo Bergman, secretary to the Stones at the time, described the film of the Circus: "Everybody was involved in it, but it just never got finished. There are some nice things in it, but musically it doesn't hold up." Since Brian was a member of the Stones, he had to participate in the Circus. He could barely whisper his line, "Here come the clowns." People who were there described him as pathetic. This was his last performance as a Rolling Stone.

The Rolling Stones Rock and Roll Circus *TV show.* L–R: *John Lennon, Yoko Ono, Keith Richard, Mick Jagger, Charlie Watts,* **Brian,** *and Bill Wyman.*

Brian was always trying to figure things out. I presume he got to the point where he asked himself questions and couldn't understand his answers. He tied himself in a knot, a very brittle knot. I think if you would have untied the knot, the rope would have fallen to pieces, in millions of little fragments.

— Alexis Korner

Brian and Suki Potier visited Arthur C. Clarke (author of *2001, A Space Odyssey*) whom Brian had met earlier through mutual friends, and his brother in Ceylon over the 1968 Christmas holiday. "Brian was very different in Ceylon," Suki said, "He got himself together. He even played with a local group on stage. He fought two fights for me, which I was amazed at. These men had been fancying me and Brian got really jealous."

Brian returned to London, looking tanned and healthy, in time for his appeal on January 13, 1969. Lord Parker again presided over the hearing. Although the trial judge had dismissed Brian's appeal, Lord Parker said that no doubt the trial judge expected Brian to be cleared: " . . . his sentence which included a breach of probation, reflects the fact that he [the trial judge] felt that this young man might well have been acquitted."

Brian's attorney, Michael Havers, said that because the jury might be prejudiced, their verdict was not objective. "The twelve men and women," Havers said, "were faced with a bizarre young man who had long hair and had made a great deal of money at an early age—a situation in which inherent prejudice is very likely to occur. This is what happens when there are jurors of an age group which feels very strongly about a young man of this kind."

At the trial, police said they had found one-third of an ounce of cannabis in a ball of wool in Brian's apartment. Brian denied knowing anything about the ball of wool. He had been a temporary tenant, living in the apartment for only two weeks. Mr. Havers stated that the evidence was weak and that the court should have a "lurking doubt," particularly since the trial judge had already expressed his doubts about the result. Brian was acquitted.

Several weeks earlier, Brian had purchased an eleven-acre country home, Cotchford Farm, for 31,500 pounds. The house, about fifty miles southeast of London on the edge of Ashdown Forest, had previously belonged to A.A. Milne, author of *Winnie the Pooh*. (Centuries before, the farm had reportedly housed William the Conqueror.) Cotchford Farm, at Hartfield Sussex, has six bedrooms, three reception rooms, three bathrooms, garages, a staff apartment, and a heated swimming pool. A sundial with carved figures of Eeyore, Pooh, Piglet stands in the garden. In the corner of the garden, marooned among clusters of multicolored flowers, stands a life-size statue of Christopher Robin. The idyllic setting helped soften and soothe Brian. "He was so proud of the house," Alexis Korner said, "because of Pooh. He was knocked out. He thought it was marvelous to go up to the sundial and realize that there were buried manuscripts of *Winnie the Pooh* there. He was very proud of the sundial and often walked around it. It's the same part of Brian that liked lying on his back on the springboard over the swimming pool because all the blues and greens felt like Sweden. It took him a long time to find the right blue to paint a couple of walls and a ceiling in the house. He was looking for the same sort of blue that he had seen in Morocco. That was very important to him, indeed."

Dr. Green felt that Brian's buying Cotchford Farm was another attempt of his to get inside someone else's fantasy, "It was never his, I'm sure. It wasn't a creative thing buying Winnie the Pooh's house. If he had gone up to the Pyrenees or the Whatchamacallit Mountains where he went to record his Arabs, and found himself a broken-down castle or fort and turned it into the best goddamned, most luxurious place then that would have been his. But he wasn't ready for it. He was scared . . . he really wasn't breaking out.

"I'm talking about things which were his, and his own 'outside' of the sort of fantasy world in which he, perforce, lived as a pop star. I'm sure a large number of people in the pop star world are capable of being two people at the same time if their entourage, their followers, would allow them to be. Some of them have more personality than Brian did, in that sense, but surely it's possible for someone in that world, if he has some real identity in the sense of a formed personality, to go home nights and have something else— and not be dependent all the time on the Milky Way."

Although Brian still lived mainly in London, he would go down to Cotchford for weekends, often with Suki, David Bailey (the *Vogue* photographer), and Penelope Tree, a model. Brian vacillated between his role as a country squire, resting in front of the fire with dogs and cats at his feet, and his role as a pop star, behaving wildly and raving it up in London. Long, mid-evening country walks would sometimes help to stabilize that devastating dichotomy. "Brian started changing and getting much better," Suki said, "off the use of so many sleeping pills and tranquilizers. Then the Stones' situation would come back to him like, 'My God, am I leaving or not?' He started drinking, getting worse and worse and that's when I split. I said that I'd come back when he wasn't a pop star anymore."

While in London, Brian would spend many evenings club-hopping. His appearance suffered greatly from all the strain he had been under. Alexis remembers Brian showing up at the Revolution (a club), "looking like Louis the Fourteenth mummified! Brian wore even more foppish clothes than usual, and he put on some very unhealthy fat—like the cats who drink too much, and their faces go white and puffy and pockmarked. He had gotten a bit of a gut as well."

Alexis, who was working for the BBC, happened to interview Mick a few days after running into Brian. "I can't remember," Alexis said, "exactly what Mick said, but it boiled down to the fact that 'Brian's in a bad way. Would you please get in touch with him because maybe he would like to talk to you.' They were having trouble talking to Brian. They felt Brian could do with someone to talk to who wasn't trying to get something out of him. Mick *was* concerned about Brian. He didn't let on much to anyone. I was surprised because Mick has always concealed himself very much from everyone."

Mick solicited Alexis' help . . . because he and Brian had been friends for so long, but especially because of Alexis' fatherly role to all the British blues artists. "I was responsible for Brian, to a certain extent," Alexis said, "because I made it possible for him to come into this business. And my feelings for Brian were mixed between a personal affection, personal dislike, an enormous responsibility."

Shortly after seeing Mick, Alexis phoned Brian and was

disturbed to hear a very frightened Brian describe his immediate surroundings. He whispered to Alexis that he was being kept in the house and watched and wasn't allowed out except for certain times of the day. He hoped maybe Alexis could sneak in and visit him.

Alexis, sometimes bringing his wife and daughter, began to visit Brian. Alexis felt he would benefit from seeing a stable family situation. The visits, which lasted four or five hours, were mostly spent talking. Yet, a few hours after the Korners had returned to their London home, Brian would phone and complain about certain chauffeurs locking him in the house and making sure he couldn't go anywhere. Brian grew more adamant about his fears in his last weeks. As to whether these were Brian's distortions or reality, one will never know. Both are equally possible.

Brian always enjoyed playing host to the Korners—sitting at the head of the table and pouring wine for the guests and himself. Brian often drank considerable amounts of wine until he fell asleep. The conversation usually centered on music. Brian mentioned that he wanted to produce Alexis' daughter's recordings, and talked vaguely about song fragments he had written in Morocco. A few bitter complaints were directed at the absent Stones who never recorded his songs. Whenever the song, "Ballad of John and Yoko" (with lyrics referring to the crucifixion) played, Brian gave a hoarse laugh.

"Brian liked to talk about the fringes of metaphysics," Alexis said. "He was very interested in extrasensory perception, but for very short periods of time. He was interested in Buddhism, although I think he was more interested in the paraphernalia than the philosophy. Oh, he loved paraphernalia. One day we went round opening chests and pulling out clothes and tapestries that he bought all over the place. He loved the panoply and all the decorations around religion."

Brian wanted to return to the first music that moved him—the blues. His overriding desire was to form a band and play music that combined traditional jazz (with Brian playing soprano sax in the style of Sidney Bechet), rhythm 'n' blues, gospel, and Moroccan music. Alexis remained convinced that Brian wanted to return to *his* musical roots because he felt that the Stones were cheating, musically. "Whenever I talked to Brian," Alexis said, "and we'd meet at odd times—like when Jimmy Reed was at the Flamingo or when Rufus Thomas was playing somewhere—we'd always end up talking about jazz.

"Brian wanted to start something else which had nothing to do with what he'd done with the Rolling Stones. He wanted it to just be him."

Brian very much wanted his East Grinstead neighbors to accept him. He'd spend many evenings in the Haywagon Pub, down the road from his house, playing bar-billiards with the locals. He never flaunted his wealth in the pub, although he wore his characteristic tight velvet trousers and silk shirts. In the spring of 1969, Brian told Dennis, the barman, that he was worried about upsetting his neighbors because his land was a bit overgrown. He didn't want his neighbors to think he was a hippie. Brian wanted to put up a fence that day and had gathered all the necessary materials. He had tried to get some men to put it up, but no one was available until the following week. Finally Brian asked Dennis if he could persuade his friends to put up the fence. Dennis rounded up some men and they finished the fence that day, much to Brian's relief.

One evening, a drunken Brian left the Haywagon, got on his Triumph motorcycle and crashed into the window of the town's grocery shop. He was terrified that dope would be planted on him. Several local friends took him—under a false name—to be patched up at a hospital.

On an afternoon in June, Mick and Keith went down to Cotchford to see if Brian wanted to start touring again with the Rolling Stones. The Stones really wanted to go on the road soon and perform live. As Mick said in an interview by Roy Carr in *Creem* magainze (July, 1974): "What we didn't like was that we wanted to play on stage and Brian wasn't in any condition to play. He was far too messed up in his mind to play. . . . I don't think he wanted to and it was this that pissed me off. He didn't have the desire to go on stage. . . ."

This was the last time Keith and Mick saw Brian. " . . .[Brian] said, 'I can't do it again. I can't start again and go on the road again like that. I don't think I can go to America and do those one-nighters anymore. I just can't.' And we said, 'We understand. We'll come and see you in a couple weeks and see how you feel. Meantime, how do you want to say it? Do you want to say that you've left?' And he said, 'Yeah, let's do it. Let's say I've left and if I want I can come back.' "

" 'Because we've got to know. We've got to take your place because we're starting to think about getting it together for another tour. We've got itchy feet and we've got Mick Taylor lined up.' We didn't really, we didn't have Mick waiting in the wings to bring on. But we wanted to know if we should get someone else or if Brian wanted to get back into it again."

Brian told his father that since he was unable to go to America because of his drug conviction, the band had decided to drop him from the group. Brian phoned his father one day before the news appeared to say that the break from the Stones wasn't permanent. It was only due to the American tour and that he would rejoin them for a European tour in 1970.

Brian's official press statement read: "The music Mick Jagger and Keith Richard have been writing has progressed at a tangent as far as my own taste is concerned." But as Keith said, "You don't leave the Stones singing, you just get carried out."

Great secrecy surrounded Brian's leaving the Stones. Rumors abounded. "Mick was tending to put Brian down, dismissing him as a little boy who didn't even know what he wanted," Peter Jones said. "Andrew had been interviewed by countless people in an effort to find out what was going on." Then one June afternoon Brian strolled into the 142 Club where he used to drink with Peter Jones. Brian, looking parchment white and sickly, sported a toothy grin—as if to say, "He knew he had done something disastrous career-wise and even though he was not too sure of the outcome, he was glad he did it." Brian told Peter he wanted to produce records. He had contacted some artists that he wanted to work with (Elke Brooks was one). Many artists contacted Brian asking him to play on their records or to produce them. Brian told Peter that he finally felt he could call his life his own. "Personally, I think there would not have been any holding Brian back once he'd really found his feet on his own," Peter Jones said, "because he contributed so much, early on, to the Stones."

While living at Cotchford, Brian radiated excitement about the band he was forming. Ian Stewart described him: "It was almost like somebody had taken a big weight off his shoulders. He had Alexis down there, John Mayall, Micky Waller, Mitch Mitchell . . . they'd all been down playin'. In fact he was on to me to go down there and play but I said, 'I've started one group with you and that's enough.' "

Brian's main help and source of support during these band-forming weeks was Alexis. Originally Brian wanted to play with him, but he refused. Instead, Alexis helped form the band's musical direction. "Brian was happy at that time," Alexis said, "because he was into doing things, which is *the* up. Brian and I were phoning each other all the time and saying, 'What do you think of so and so? Or should we try so and so?' We were getting into a sort of unit of musicians together down there to see whether they were the right ones. He wasn't at all afraid of getting together with musicians again."

Alexis' own band, New Church, was soon leaving to tour Germany. Brian wanted to join the band even to tour. Brian had come to hate touring with the Rolling Stones, rehearsing and playing "their music" over and over. But with his own band, however, the idea of a tour was exciting. He wanted to get out on the road again. Alexis, at first, said, "Definitely! I finally said, 'No,' because I really didn't think that I could accept the responsibility of looking after Brian on the road, knowing what he was like. Especially in Germany—where for a long time it was Brian Jones and the Rolling Stones, rather than Mick Jagger and the Rolling Stones. Brian was enormously popular in Germany and I was a bit worried. I felt we'd have to have security and I didn't think I could cope with that. . . .So I said, 'No thank you, but as soon as I come back, we'll start working with the band.' But he wanted to go on the road. In fact, he reckoned that six months from the start of rehearsals, at the most, his band would be ready to go.

"Brian was a positive communicator. You watched Brian. I think he put out, a word I use reluctantly, tremendously powerful vibes. My wife remembers very clearly one day when we were down at Cotchford, Brian saying how much he wanted to get back on stage and on the road. While he was talking he was rushing around the room banging a tambourine to emphasize words; a back-on-stage thing again. I think he was happiest playing the tambourine. He loved the aggressive sharpness and edgy attacking thing of the tambourine—when you rush up and slap it in someone's face. And Brian liked moving suddenly and sharply.

"Brian told us, 'I want to get up there and put the boot to 'em, put the boot to 'em.' [This] is an English expression for kicking someone to death. It was also [as much] an aggression against people at the same time. And this is the trip he was very much into.

"I had great affection for Brian and even more than that I had a great fear for Brian . . . I think that there are certain people who are driven in a way that they are ultimately unable to control. They are bound to die very young because the amount of times that you risk yourself must be limited. If you never exercise any self-restraint you come to the end of your chances. It was so edgy all the time with Brian. He veered by a hundred percent. You really had to follow very, very closely what was happening—otherwise if you relaxed you were lost in a couple of seconds. Brian was very sensitive. He could feel vibes which weren't there at all—maybe my perceptions were duller."

In those last few week, sycophants invaded Cotchford. Brian shelled out the money and the dope to ward off the loneliness. Keith described the scene: "Hangers-on. Buying them booze, out by the pool, sort of *La Dolce Vita* . . . for the companionship."

During Brian's last three weeks, June 17 to July 3 1969, he lived with the Swedish Anna Wohlin, his latest girlfriend, who was twenty-three; Janet Lawson, a nurse; and Frank Throgood, a forty-four year old builder. Janet and Frank lived in the guest apartment above the garage.

People who knew Frank thought he was a rather nefarious character, and why Brian employed him was unclear. "Brian said that Frank was taking him for a ride," Alexis said, "—charging him for work that wasn't being done. [Brian] took me around the house and deliberately showed me bits of the house he had paid to have done that were . . .

Anna Wohlin who was living with him at the time of his death. July, 1969.

a couple of thousand pounds here, eight hundred pounds there, that hadn't been done and he'd been charged for it. . . . I suppose there's a part of Brian that would let Frank go on doing it. Otherwise Frank would have had some incredible hold over Brian, which seems unlikely." Christopher Gibbs said, "[Frank] was taking Brian for the most incredible series of rides and hanging around there with his friends getting drunk all the time. Brian was aware of that kind of thing, but liked having friendly people nearby. People he couldn't conceivably regard as the enemy—because he got very paranoid after his busts."

Brian Jones Dies in Pool; Was 'Rolling Stones' Star

LONDON (AP) — Brian Jones, 26-year-old pop music idol who rose to stardom as one of Britain's Rolling Stones, died today while taking a midnight swim... er... about 20 minutes went into the house. "Wh... went for...

im at his Hartfield home... good...

manager...

Pop Idol Found De in His Po

HARTFIELD, Engl midnight swim -clad Swedish b in death yest ormer Rolling Jones—a o n e - t e collector and a ssistant who bec idol of millions. rate life-saving ld after Jones v the bottom of t g pool at his 15t Sussex farmhou wn Forest, south

red that Jones, 27 d the equivalen week, may have an attack of asth rt attack caused eral use of an lant. An inhaler beside the 50 l.

rted from the s last month nded to form o and play his usic.

night, Jones n, 22, went them was a rank Thoro-

ack bikini, house after ogood fol tes later. hortly aft per

Rolling Stone Jones Found Dead in Pool

HARTFIELD, England — (UPI) — Pop guitarist Brian Jones, who quit the Rolling Stones group last month was found dead in the swimming pool of his $72,000 home early today. He was 26.

Police and the Sussex County coroner were investigating the death of the shaggy blond-haired pop star who left the Stones after a clash over music styles with leader Mick Jagger.

"It is possible that Brian had an attack of asthma while he was bathing," said Tom Keylock, tour manager for the Rolling Stones.

Friends pulled Jones from the pool and called an ambulance. Attendants tried artificial resuscitation but he was dead when a doctor arrived at his 16th Century home, formerly owned by Winnie the Pooh author A. A. Milne.

JONES

Jones had been a member of the pop group since it was formed in 1962 and as its records, such as "Let's Spend the Night Together" and "Satisfaction" hit the top of the charts, selling 43,000,000.

When Jones left the Rolling Stones on June 9 he issued a statement saying "the music of Mick Jagger and Keith Richard has, to my mind, progressed on a tangent as far as my own tastes are concerned."

After watching Rowan and Martin's Laugh-In last

Mystery surrounds Brian's death. Newspaper accounts differ about significant facts. Many friends I spoke to had their own death theories. All newspaper stories contained the same information concerning the early events of that hot July evening. Brian and Anna had been drinking and watching TV. At around 10 P.M., Brian went to the apartment above the garage and asked Janet and Frank to join them. Frank later told the coroner that when Brian came to his flat, "he was not really under the influence of drink but he staggered slightly. . . . We had quite a bit to drink." Between them they drank almost an entire bottle of brandy, two-thirds of a bottle of vodka, a half-bottle of whiskey, and some wine. Janet attempted conversation with Brian but found his speech garbled because he had had his "sleepers." Janet believed these to be sleeping pills. Brian decided to go for a swim to cool off. (Brian swam very well. George Chkiantz and Brian had gone swimming in Tangier just one year earlier. "Brian swam out to sea . . ." George said. "Suki and I sort of paddled around. Brian came back the minute he saw me and Suki in the water and he said, 'Be careful! The current's really strong at the moment.' But Brian was already swimming quite far out. The coast guard was obviously a bit jumpy because somebody *was* swimming in what was obviously a very hard current. Brian swam back quite firmly and strongly against the current. It was obvious that Brian wasn't the best swimmer that I've ever seen, but he was obviously capable of going more or less indefinitely in the water.")

Janet Lawson said that she warned Brian not to swim: "Both Brian and Frank were in no fit condition to swim. I mentioned it to the men but they disregarded the warning." Brian had trouble raising himself onto the springboard, so Frank helped him. According to Janet Lawson: "The two men appeared sluggish in the water but I gathered they could look after themselves." Anna had returned to the house. "Brian was swimming quite normally," Frank said. "After about twenty minutes I got out of the water and went to the house for a cigarette [another article quotes this as "a towel"]. Brian was quite all right then. I had seen him swimming like this before and thought it was all right to leave him." In one newspaper account Miss Lawson "returned to the pool and saw Brian lying quite motionless . . .[she] suspected the worst. She screamed, 'Something's happened to Brian!' " Another account said that Frank came back out to the pool and saw Brian at the bottom and called to Anna. Accounts agree that Anna and Frank dragged Brian out of the water whereupon Janet pumped a little water out of him and massaged his chest for fifteen minutes. Anna gave him the "kiss of life, suddenly felt his hand grip hers, and then there was no other movement."

Dr. Albert Sachs, consultant pathologist at Queen Victoria Hospital, performed the autopsy. He described Brian's liver as twice the normal weight and in an "advanced state of fatty degeneration," and his heart was larger than it should have been for a man his age. Dr. Sachs also found evidence of chronic bronchial trouble and believed that Brian once suffered from pleurisy. He found no evidence of Brian's experiencing an asthma attack that night. He stated that Brian's death was due to drowning associated with ingestion of alcohol, drugs, and severe liver degeneration. Brian's blood alcohol was .140 milligrams per hundred, and a urine test showed that there were .172 milligrams of an amphetamine substance in his body, a large quantity of the drug. And the verdict: misadventure.

Looking back, Keith felt that the combination of barbiturates and alcohol was devastating: "His asthma was psychosomatic. The thing was that Brian was taking so many

Tuinal, barbiturates, and Mandrax. He used all the old tricks. He'd pierce the end of it so the barbiturate would pop out that much quicker; he wouldn't have to wait for it to dissolve. He was always heavy into whiskey and that's a fatal combination over a period of time. The thing about all barbiturates is that once you're into them, you can't remember how many you've taken. You forget. Half an hour ago you already dropped three and you hit them up again. Diving into a swimming pool full of booze and barbiturates, you really have to assume that somebody has to only get hurt. . . . There's so many stories [about what happened when Brian died] that none of them sounded authentic because they just didn't tie in there."

Part of the rock 'n' roll mythology that has grown since Brian's death concerns the many death theories that have emerged—some believable, some fantastic: Keith hid in the bushes and then pushed Brian into the pool; the Mafia held Brian underwater because he knew too much about the Stones' finances; Brian, with much preparation, committed suicide. George Chkiantz thought Brian died from a seizure similar to the one he had witnessed that night in Tangier: "Brian had taken some drink and probably had one of those paralysis things, fell straight into the swimming pool because he happened to be standing by it. The seizure would have been all right on dry land. I can't see how other people in the house failed to notice what happened to their host. There was probably too much dope in the house to risk calling the police—and so they probably just ran." Ian Stewart thought that Brian's "death was accidental. . . . Most likely thing was he was drunk and he fell into the pool. He was a good swimmer you know, swam very well actually. But he was probably drunk and he got into the pool and there were all these people down there sittin' drinkin' his booze and nobody around that could actually do anything when they were needed."

A strange twist came from Jim Carter-Fae, the manager of The Speakeasy, who knew Anna Wohlin before she met Brian: "The night Brian died I got a call from Anna, maybe about ten minutes after it happened. Somebody got the phone and put it down and she called me a bit later. Anna was very upset. She was moved out of the country and told to say nothing—so fast it wasn't true. I don't know who made her do this. Anna told me she had never seen Brian as happy as he was the night he died, with the way things were going with the band. She said that she had gone upstairs to sleep, then suddenly she came down. Frank and the nurse were standing by the pool, Brian was there and they weren't doing anything at all. Anna dived in and tried to fish him out. Brian was floating underwater in the pool and they wouldn't help her at all. They were just standing by the pool watching. And after that Anna said *everything* disappeared from the house.

The house and swimming pool where Brian Jones died on July 3, 1969.

The funeral. Mr. and Mrs. Lewis Jones, daughter Barbara (left), and Suki. July 10, 1969.

After Brian died many of his belongings mysteriously vanished from Cotchford. "I know that things got nicked," Keith said. "Harem screens down at Brian's place were there when Mick and I went down to see him about leaving the band, and two weeks later they weren't there. . . ."

Two of the Stones (Bill and Charlie), Suki, Linda Lawrence, and Julian attended Brian's funeral in Cheltenham, at the church where Brian had been a choir-boy. Among those missing were Mick, Keith, and Anita. (Mick was in Australia to film *Ned Kelly*.) After the funeral, Linda was asked back to the Jones' home and Mrs. Jones held Julian close to her. Linda placed this Japanese poem on her wreath of forget-me-nots:

> Now my loneliness
> Following
> The fireworks—
> Look! A falling star!

E P I L O G U E

THE SUBSEQUENT FATE OF SOME OF THE OTHER major participants in this tragedy makes one wonder about the existence of a greater morality. Keith's drug problems have been well-documented. Anita Pallenberg has had her share of suffering: Keith left her for a younger woman; a young man shot himself in her bed; her physical appearance has altered so dramatically that she has become virtually unrecognizable. Suki Potier recently died. Linda Lawrence married Donovan Leitch, the singer-songwriter and is bringing up three children, one of whom is singing and recording. Julian Lawrence, Brian and Linda's son, lives with Linda. He is a healthy eighteen-year-old who traveled with the Rolling Stones on their last tour.

The legacy of Brian Jones lives on. The "Brian Jones Memorial Fan Club," an international organization, continues to keep Brian's thousands of fans informed and his spirit alive. **Through these fans, Brian Jones will never die.**